UNSTOPPABLE LIFE

Beginning of the Journey – S.R. Costa Photography

UNSTOPPABLE LIFE

The Way to a Happier You
Learn to Ride the Wave Instead of Fighting the Tide.

Written by
Kat and Steve Sanders

Lionsgate
Publishing

Photos by RS Costa Photography and Kat Sanders

Illustrations by Steve Sanders

Edited by Kristi Abshire Sanders

Lionsgate Publishing

18851 Bardeen Ave, Suite 200

Irvine CA, 92612

www.lionsgatepublishing.com

Printed in the United States of America

First printing September 20, 2010

ISBN: 978-0-615-40812-5

www.theunstoppablelife.com

INTRODUCTION - WHY WE WROTE THIS BOOK............................ 7

A GOOD DAY GONE BAD.. 7
WHAT IS THIS BOOK ABOUT?.. 9
    It's in the Bag – Kat's Cat Nemo –Kat Sanders......................... 9
ABOUT KAT AND STEVE.. 10
CONCLUDING THE INTRODUCTION: 11
THE SERENITY PRAYER 12
STEVE'S FINAL WORDS FROM ICU 12
UNSTOPPABLE... 14
    Resting Elephant Seals.. 15

CHAPTER ONE – THE HISTORY AND MEDICAL SIDE 16

LIFE CHANGING EVENTS 16
WHAT HAPPENED TO ME 17
    AVM 18
    Life is a Beach... 25
    Kat's Craniotomy... 29

CHAPTER TWO – GOOD & BAD HAPPEN TO GOOD PEOPLE 35

MIRACLE 10 35
WHO IS REALLY IN CONTROL?.. 35
    Minding the Tide.. 37
WHY DO BAD THINGS HAPPEN TO GOOD PEOPLE?................... 39
ELEPHANT SEAL BULL - 42

CHAPTER THREE – WHAT'S IMPORTANT? 43

WHAT IS RIGHT FOR MY LIFE? 43
WHAT MAKES US HAPPY? 46
    Corona Del Mar Crane... 47
SMALL 48
SAFETY – BASIC HUMAN NEEDS 49
FOOD.. 50
WATER.. 50
CLOTHING 51
SHELTER 53
GETTING INVOLVED 53
WHAT MAKES YOU HAPPY? 54
    Can You See Me?... 54

CHAPTER FOUR – MORALITY MATTERS...................................... 55

MORALITY, FORGIVENESS, RESPECT AND MANNERS.................... 55
TRUE WINNERS 56
MORALITY 57
    Kat and Steve Renew Their Wedding Vows 59

CHAPTER FIVE – FORGIVENESS AND GRACE.............................. 60

FORGIVENESS 60
GRACE 65

CHAPTER SIX – RESPECT AND MANNERS 68

RESPECT 68
MANNERS 70

CHAPTER SEVEN – ACHIEVE AND BE HAPPY 72

ATTITUDE, ACHIEVEMENT, LEGACY AND SATISFACTION 72
ATTITUDE 72
ACHIEVEMENT 74
NO EXCUSES 74
LEGACY 75
SATISFACTION 77
  A Norman Rockwell Day at the Beach – Kat Sanders 79

CHAPTER EIGHT – IS IT LOVE? 80

LOVE, SUBSERVIENCE, SACRIFICE AND SPIRITUALITY 80
LOVE 80
SUBSERVIENCE 83
SACRIFICE 84
SPIRITUALITY 85
  Kat, Son Matt and Brandy in Pismo Beach 87

CHAPTER NINE – WHAT DO YOU KNOW? 88

LEARNING AND KNOWLEDGE 88
FOUR WARNING CAVEATS ABOUT KNOWLEDGE: 89
  I'm All Ears 92

CHAPTER TEN – WHAT ARE MY CHOICES? 93

HOW TO DECIDE WHAT IS RIGHT IN MY LIFE 93
WHAT LIFE GOALS ARE NOT 93
TIME MATTERS 95
MY 10 BEST DAYS 96
  Buccaneer Queen 100

CHAPTER ELEVEN - FUN, PASSION, AND TALENTS 101

HAVING FUN 101
DRUDGERY OR CHALLENGE 102
PASSION 103
TALENT 105

CHAPTER TWELVE - EXERCISES 108

IF I WON THE LOTTERY 108
BUCKET LIST 109
MILLION BUCK GIVE AWAY 110

WHAT IS MY LEGACY? 110
TEN BEST DAYS EXERCISE... 111
WHAT AM I PASSIONATE ABOUT 111
WHAT ARE MY TALENTS? 112
YOUR COMFORT ZONE, GOALS AND LEGACY 112
THINGS I NEED TO SAY 113

CHAPTER THIRTEEN – PRIORITIES **114**

LET'S GET GOING 114
BIG ROCKS 114
NAME FIVE BIG ROCKS IN YOUR LIFE 117
THE BUCKET LIST 117
NOW DO SOMETHING! 118
   Balboa Sweet Success – Kat Sanders *119*
ACTION ITEMS.. 120

CHAPTER FOURTEEN – I'VE GOT THE IDEA. NOW WHAT?...... **121**

PATIENCE 121
PARTNERING 123
   Rules for Partnering.... *124*
   Call a Time Out... *124*
   Misunderstanding *124*
   Right Words, Wrong Words *124*
   Be a Coach, not a Mentor *124*
   Handle Conversations with Love *125*
SCHEDULING 125
   Where Do I Start? *126*
   How Far in Advance do I Plan? *126*
   Big Rocks First... *126*
   Fill in with Pebbles and Sand *127*
   Be Prepared to Make Changes *127*
HAMMER OR TOOL 128
CHECKUPS.. 129
   I'm Not Lion. Trust Me - Kat Sanders.................................... *129*

CHAPTER FIFTEEN - AFFECTING, CHANGING & ACCEPTING **130**

   Banff Springs Hotel... *133*

CHAPTER SIXTEEN – BRING IT ON HOME................................ **134**

AFTERTHOUGHTS.. 134
IT ISN'T YOUR FAULT 135
NEVER GIVE UP HOPE 135
REALITY CHECK.. 137
PRACTICING WHAT WE PREACH 137
IN A NUTSHELL 138

ACKNOWLEDGEMENTS AND THANKS.................................**139**

INTRODUCTION - Why We Wrote This Book

A Good Day Gone Bad

"My head hurts really bad and I'm scared." said my lovely wife, Kat, just before unconsciously sliding off the bed to the floor.

I managed to reach her in time to slow the fall, though I wasn't quick or strong enough to stop her descent. I let her glide softly to the carpet, arranged her body so she would be comfortable, got her some blankets to keep her warm and dialed 911.

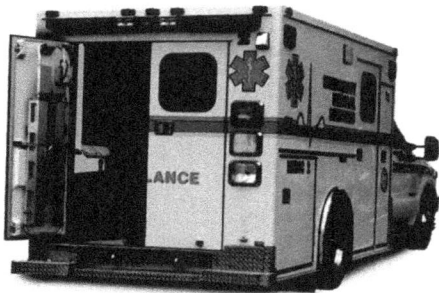

There had been no warning, no symptoms, no way to prepare. She was the picture of health, then, five minutes later, she was nearly comatose.

She is a physically attractive woman, even after the tenth time she's turned 39, but that is not the source of her beauty. She is brilliant. Even when her ideas are ridiculously better than others, she makes people feel they are important and necessary. She possesses more understanding and love than a warehouse full of teddy bears. She is no saint, none of us are, but she is as close to an angel as I have ever come.

Just that morning we attended a weekly board meeting. She felt great. No issues or pains. We arrived at the meeting slightly early for Kat . . . which meant on time. She enthusiastically announced Earth Day. She is Green certified, or certifiable, your choice. She was vibrant, witty and together; typical Kat. Now, there she was, on the floor, trying but unable to communicate.

Dispatch sent an ambulance in a matter of minutes. They rushed her to emergency. An attendant, nurse or doctor, I don't remember which, congratulated me on quick action. He said that had she arrived fifteen minutes later she would probably not have made it. Their preliminary evaluation showed bleeding on the brain. They did what they could, relieved skull pressure and reduced bleeding, saving her life, then shuttled her to a nearby community hospital where a neurological team was standing by.

After taking a CAT scan, the neuro team decided to forgo immediate surgery in favor of wait and see. She was somewhat stable, but definitely had a hemorrhaging brain. Without further tests they could not determine the source of the trauma. The next morning, after running more tests, they discovered the root of the problem, and were strategizing what to do. My beautiful wife started deteriorating rapidly. They had no choice but to perform emergency brain surgery.

All the things we planned; the trip to Europe, visits to family, seeing the Grand Canyon, and jet-skiing vanished within minutes.

We could have done them, but work commitments, both hers and mine, always seemed to take priority. Business replaced outings, shows, and lunches together. Time was a commodity much shorter in supply than we had thought and once spent, time could not be retrieved. Truth is, someone else could have done the work we instead chose to do. But, no one could spend quality time together for us. We ignorantly believed there would always be a tomorrow full of hours that we would share.

That assumption proven false, petty arguments no longer were important. . . where and what we ate, whether or not we worked out. Should we buy a new car to replace my aging steed? How could we expand and protect our business? Everything that seemed mountainous yesterday, was suddenly a molehill today. Priorities changed instantaneously.

We would not repeat the same mistakes. We would put more value on the here and now and less value on tomorrow . . . there might not be one. Instead of planning for work we would embrace fun, love and family . . . but only if she is still alive.

The above was written by my husband, Steve, in the Intensive Care Unit waiting room, while I was undergoing emergency brain surgery.

What is this book about?

This book is about learning to ride the wave instead of fighting the tide. It will help you discover your personal roadmap for life, a direction leading to greater satisfaction. It also provides a means to avoid remorse, by identifying and dodging wrong choices in the first place. It also explains how and why we should accept or forgive the poor choices we've already made. Retain and glorify the good, letting the rest go. Keep important, happy things in a mental heavy duty safe. The rest is trash to be thrown away.

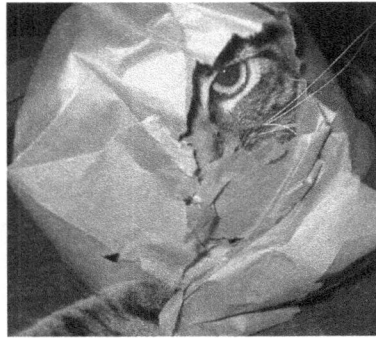

It's in the Bag – Kat's Cat Nemo –Kat Sanders

Circumstances in life are unstoppable and often unfair. Nobody said it was going to be easy. No one promised flowers, but if we find ourselves on a path surrounded by blossoms, we should pause to appreciate their beauty and perfume. Life occasionally sucks, no matter who you are or what direction you have chosen. The only thing we have control over is how we deal with it.

The best things in life often occur when we least expect them. How can we predict the moment we will meet a soul mate or rescue the best pet from the shelter or get that great job opportunity? We cannot know, good or bad, what is coming. The power to choose can either magnify the good or glorify the bad, but the notion that we can change what is unchangeable or know enough to know what the universe has in store for us is silly. We have to make the best of what we have and play the cards we are dealt. The many and clichéd ways of expressing this same sentiment prove it to be an altruism worthy of exploration.

Whether or not the afterlife exists, learning to better understand and accept the life we've been given garners more peace and happiness than fighting every outcome. Learning to pick battles we must, instead of fighting them all, will result in important victories and greater self-esteem. Our time and strength are limited. Both must be spent in ways that achieve rather than sidetrack our goals.

Those reading this book in hopes of learning how to control their life will be sadly disappointed. This book is about improving your quality of life, not by learning how to control it, but by learning how to better accept, manage and survive it.

About Kat and Steve

Kat and Steve Sanders, the authors of this book, are neither mental health professionals nor trained social workers. Aside from the occasional college undergrad class, we have no formal training in behavioral science.

What we DO have is direct personal experience in life-changing crisis. My near-death Arterio-Venous Malformation (AVM) surgery in the brain, and subsequent recovery, taught us both much about the art of living. We are writing this book to clarify for ourselves, and hopefully for others, what we have learned.

Steve and I are fairly well read and, as instructors, have learned to draw from the wisdom of others. There will be a few selected quotes, and we will appreciatively give credit where credit is due. There won't be much plagiarism, but artistic license and imagination are liberally applied. Some of the stories are true, some are made up, you get to choose which is which.

We draw from the wisdom of Tony Robbins, ("Unlimited Power"), John Wooden ("Pyramid of Success"), Robert Fulghum ("All I Really Need to Know I Learned in Kindergarten"), Mark

Twain, Will Rogers, Jack Canfield (Chicken Soup for the Soul), Zig Ziglar, Gary Keller (Quantum Leap), religious transcripts and books, and other motivational characters, trainers and authors we have had the good fortune to either learn from or meet.

Concluding the Introduction:

Brotherhood, The Golden Rule, and Love are included in every belief, every philosophy, regardless of its title. There is too much wisdom in all viewpoints, to be ignored.

Regardless of whether your God is Allah, God, or Mother Nature there is commonality. There may not be a rule, but there is at very least an outline, for how life should be lived. Life is enhanced, augmented and better understood through meditation, prayer, Zen, or personal reflection.

There is power in positive thinking, no matter what it is called. There is power in people thinking good thoughts or praying to a supreme being for the benefit of others.

Even for those who do not believe in power outside themselves, prayers can help. Knowing that thousands of people had me in their thoughts made me fight harder to survive and recover. I didn't want to let them down. It gave me a strength I would not otherwise have had. It convinced me that I was worthwhile and important.

The only school of thought with which we might take exception would be the belief that everything is accidental. Mathematical probabilities undeniably preclude chance. When there are too many coincidences in a row it can no longer be coincidence. For example, the mathematical probability of a SINGLE CELL coming about by chance is 1 to 1 followed by 340 million zeros. That is, for all intents and purposes, a mathematical impossibility.

What I experienced, my survival and recovery, I believe to be the work of power greater than myself. That combined with the power of prayer and positive thinking put me where I am. Every other option seems mathematically improbable. Based on what we have read and what doctors have told us, the chances of my survival and present cognitive level, in such a very short period of time, is a trillion to one or more.

Even if math cannot prove power beyond ourselves, wouldn't our lives be better if we lived each day to the fullest, maximizing the good, while doing our best to minimize the bad? Wouldn't we treat ourselves and others better if we acted as though today would be our last day on earth? There would be fewer parting shots. Petty disagreement would be foolish.

Steve and I subscribe to the core belief that we can affect how we feel about ourselves and others, but we must do so in the face of adversity.

The Serenity Prayer

God grant me the
Serenity to accept the things I cannot change;
Courage to change the things I can; and
Wisdom to know the difference.

Steve's Final Words from ICU

The below is the last excerpt from Steve's ICU email to all of our friends.

Many of us require a 2x4 upside the head before we will transform. Hundreds, perhaps thousands of people, who know or love Kat will be immediately affected by what happened to her. They will fall into one of three categories.

Behind door number one will be those concerned only with their own fleeting temporal life and well-being.

"It is just business", they will say or "That's life" or "That's the human condition" or "In the long run, we are all dust anyway."

They are wrong. The truth is that we have the power of choice. What we do and the choices we make always matter. When gain is the result of someone's loss, it IS personal. Benefiting at the cost of others or disdaining what is right is wrong. Instant gratification that mortgages the future can only result in long term emptiness and sorrow.

To those proclaiming that the law of the jungle prevails, there can be no peace. Nothing will ever be enough because there will still be someone or something else to conquer. Those constantly looking over their shoulder rather than trying to do what is right, will undoubtedly suffer a lonely and shallow existence.

Behind door number two will be those with heart who are saddened by Kat's story but see no reason to view or do things differently. They are destined to continue their lives unabated till tragedy befalls them or someone they love. Perhaps too late, they will realize that change would have been better, that unfinished personal business was more important than business as usual. Truth can be ignored for a while, but not forever.

Behind door number three will be people affected by what happened to my Kat. They will decide that things, even if already good, could be better. They will take actions to correct past wrongs. They will revisit what is important, they will re-examine priorities, setting them straight. They will be the reason God used my beautiful wife to affect change, even when HE was not responsible for her predicament.

We made a bad business investment a couple of years back. We were hoping to recover some, if not all, of what we lost. While we waited, our medical insurance ran out. We had already signed up for our association's group medical coverage, but it will take affect long after Kat's surgery. We are medically uncovered.

The cost of her surgery will be in the $250,000-$500,000 range. The facilities, the equipment and the skill of her doctors have been incredible and worth every penny, but it is a penny we do not have. It is likely that this will cost us all that we have worked so hard to achieve for the last twenty years. Our business will survive. Our agents will be fine, but our house and many things we thought important will be gone.

I'm not bitter. The only thing that really matters is Kat's survival and recovery.

I choose door number three. I do not yet know whether she will live or die. I cannot predict whether she will remember me or our history together, her family, her friends or all the wonderful people she has already touched. All is in God's hands. I can only tell you that, through her misfortune, I am changed and will be a better person to the best of my poor ability. Failure to do so would dishonor the message sent through Kat.

Unstoppable

Surfers learn to maneuver body and board to get the best possible result out of every wave. The wave alone decides where to go. Surfers determine how far and how artistically they will ride. Like life, they don't always get the results they want. They can either pump their fist in the air after an great ride or jump back in after a wipeout.

They don't give up. The next wave might be epic. Just because the last one was a snapper (small wave) the next might be tubular (great). They jump into the surf, paddle out to the line up and hop the next wave. With practice, they learn to catch a better ride more often. That is what Unstoppable Life is all about.

Tragedy is a given. All of us, including family and friends, will eventually die. We will suffer injury at the hands of friends and strangers alike.

Life's experiences are unstoppable. Accepting what life throws at us with a more positive, peaceful and loving attitude creates unstoppable life. Learning to enjoy the journey, no matter where it takes us, gives us more control over how we feel, making us unstoppable too. But it takes planning, effort and practice. Little of it comes naturally.

We hope readers enjoy our observations and put them to good use.

Resting Elephant Seals at Piedras Blancas – Kat Sanders

(look how small the people on the bank are compared to the seals)

CHAPTER ONE – The History and Medical Side

Life Changing Events

The below was written by Steve in an email he sent to several of the people we know, updating them on my medical progress.

The prayers seem to be working. At least the medical staff thinks so. She has been moved from ICU to a step down unit. Kat will probably be coming home on Monday, presuming the CAT scan and the physical therapy exams go well. This is all very good news, and frankly miraculous.

Now the bad news. It is unlikely that Kat will be back to work for a while. She will not be able to drive for some time, either. Her short term memory does seem to have a few glitches. Like a hard drive that is fragmented, the data is there, but hard to access at times. She is also having trouble with time, like is it 6:00 AM or PM.

Fortunately no slowness of speech, in fact a little less speech might be good . . . did I say that out loud?

There are times when she is almost childlike in questions she asks and in her concerns. This is both endearing and exhausting. Those of you who have been through the "Why" stage with children will know what I'm talking about.

After finding that we were not covered by medical insurance, our request for medical assistance has been declined by both State and Feds. Apparently we made too much money last year, even though the prospects of income without Kat working this year are slim. Fortunately, our company will be just fine as it is incorporated and our agents will continue to thrive. We have become a big family, working together even more closely after Kat's near-death experience. Unfortunately, our options are few and none seem very good financially.

We were preparing for retirement over the next few years, but now realize that is a long way off. We might have survived one or two of the fiscal catastrophes, but all combined, not good.

But, none of that really matters. I feel very blessed to have Kat alive and back with us. We will survive and will live life much differently from now on. My fervent hope is that all of you learn from this. Unless you are already a saint, change the way you view your life and how you treat those you hold most dear. Do it today. Don't count on a tomorrow that may never arrive.

I love and appreciate you all. Keep the prayers a comin'.

What Happened to Me

If you don't want to know the medical details, skip this and go onto the next chapter. For those with morbid curiosity, or an interest in AVM's this is a chapter you won't want to miss.

Earlier in the morning, Steve and I had attended a weekly breakfast meeting. I reminded everyone that it was Earth Day. I am a Greenie who dislikes the waste that paper creates, while Steve is more logical and interested in the efficiency of paperless systems. I don't chain myself to trees and focus mostly on corporate waste and recycling, but Earth Day is usually an important day for me.

I had no idea how important the day would become. I was fine. I felt good and strong. Migraines that occasionally hindered my day were absent. It was a good day.

We went home to change, as I was scheduled to do some training that afternoon. I was putting on my pants when a sharp pain struck the right side of my head. I had to lie down on the bed.

I had no idea that I had an Arterio-Venous Malformation (AVM) in my brain, a birth defect. Spaghetti-like arteries were feeding directly to veins with no intervening capillaries to disburse blood to that particular part of the brain. For all intents and purposes, that part of the brain was dead. AVM's can appear anywhere in the body, arms, legs, liver, but approximately 50% of them, mine included, are in the brain.

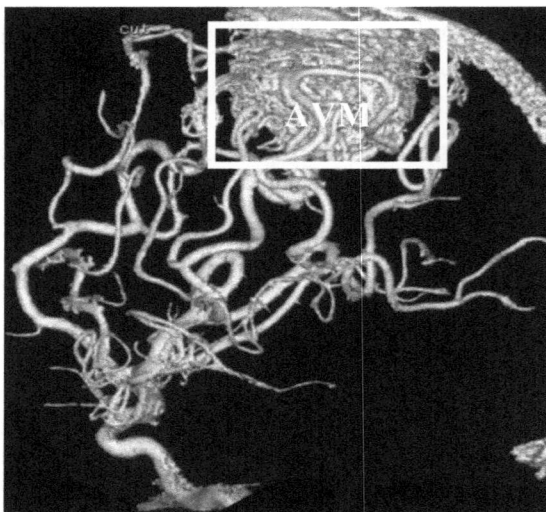

AVM

My AVM was a little bigger than a golf ball, located in the right temporal parietal region, which affects depth perception and how we deal with numbers. I also had a 2mm aneurism elsewhere. One of the weaker vascular connections gave way, causing severe bleeding to the brain. I remember saying "My head hurts really bad and I'm scared."

The symptoms were obvious and frightening. According to Steve, one minute I was healthy and salient, the next I was on the floor, barely able to move or speak.

When Steve said he was calling 911, I had presence of mind enough to remember that we were in a 30 day waiting period in which we were not covered by medical insurance, so I offered "We can't afford it."

"Screw that," he replied, dialed 911 anyway and said "My wife is having a stroke."

I don't remember much after that. Thank heaven he was home and insistent. Miracle number one.

The emergency response people did not take my condition as seriously as he did. They arrived quickly, but after conducting preliminary triage, they tried to convince him it was just a severe migraine. Steve told them that he had witnessed many migraines before and this was no migraine.

They asked who our insurance carrier was and Steve replied Kaiser. Kaiser had been our medical coverer before and we were signed up to be with them again. Coverage was not yet in place but his answer saved my life. I'll explain how later, but this was the beginning of <u>miracle number two</u>.

The firemen carried me downstairs to the ambulance and he followed me in our car. Still believing it to be a migraine, they took me to Kaiser Emergency. There were no sirens or flashing lights. They safely, and somewhat slowly, got me to the ER.

The ER staff, after one quick look, decided my condition was far more serious, and immediately put me on medications designed to relieve swelling and bleeding in my brain. They medically induced coma to prevent seizures or motion related injury.

At that particular time, Kaiser did not have an available neurological team, they were probably saving someone else's life. The Regional Hospital had a neurological team standing by. They put me back in the ambulance to transport me where they could best help.

One of the ER attendants congratulated Steve on quick action. Had I been fifteen minutes later, he claimed, I would not have made it. Completion of <u>miracle number two</u>. Had they driven me directly to Riverside County Regional Medical Center (Regional), thirty minutes further away, I probably would have died en route.

Onto Riverside County Regional Medical Center. Unfortunately, Regional had no room for me. There had been a gang fight earlier in the evening and the Intensive Care Unit (ICU) was full. Kaiser staff did their best to convince the Regional administrator to do what he could to help.

The administrator instructed them to put me in the ambulance and bring me over. He believed he could find a room for me before I arrived. Had they not found room, I would have died.

I arrived sooner than expected and Regional staff immediately put me into the Emergency Room (ER). While they were unloading me, one of the men wounded in the gang fight died, making room for me in ICU. Miracle number three.

Regional medical staff took me into ICU for observation and treatment. They drilled a vent into my skull to relieve pressure and swelling. The greatest dangers in brain trauma, outside the impact or injury itself, are additional bleeding or swelling.

Bleeding causes clotting, which can impair brain function. Swelling pushes the brain around, which can injure the brain stem, causing paralysis. Swelling also presses the brain against the skull, causing "bruising" which can affect all kinds of motor skills and memory. All are bad.

The chief neurosurgeon told Steve that they wanted to run some tests. They knew the brain was bleeding, but they didn't know exactly where the bleeding started. Without knowing the source and exact location, it was difficult to determine the best treatment. If the hemorrhage was deep in the brain, treatment options were very limited. If closer to the surface, treatment could be more aggressive. Whichever the case, I was stable. Miracle number four.

Steve stayed the night. Our daughter, living nearer to us in Southern California, and son, living out of state in the Air Force, joined him as soon as they could. Three of my closest work friends, Rebecca, Mike and Maureen, also arrived to provide support. Steve, usually an optimist by nature, called my sister and told her that she and my brother should get here as quickly as possible. Even Steve was not sure I would make it and wanted family to be as near as possible, just in case.

My sister, Cher, and brother, Ken, arranged flights from Washington State, but would not arrive till the next afternoon.

Cher notified my wonderful Aunt Beth. My Mom and Dad had passed away a few short years before, so there was no one else to call.

Early the next morning the chief neurosurgeon came to get Steve. Things are never good when a husband is taken aside for special counsel with a doctor.

"We ran the die tests while she was stable," started the doctor, "And we have discovered the cause of the bleeding. There is a malformation on the right side that has ruptured. Though she was initially stable, she is now deteriorating rapidly. We need to operate immediately. **This is as bad as it gets**."

"There are other options," finished the doctor.

"What are those?" queried Steve.

"Well . . . ," the doctor hesitated, "We could elect not to operate and see what happens, but she might die without treatment."

"As I said," answered Steve, forcing a rhetorical smile. "What are the options?"

The doctor smiled back, appreciative that Steve understood the critical nature of the situation. Hubby signed the consent forms and it was off to the races. Well . . . not exactly off to the races, but onto surgery.

They opened up approximately a third of my skull, carefully removing the pieces so they could be re-inserted if the operation was a success. Fortunately, they discovered that the AVM was in the brain near the surface. There would be no need for digging through the brain to find it. <u>Miracle five</u>.

AVM's can be treated in several ways, but the most common surgical methods are tying off or removal. With deeper AVM's in which surgery may cause as much damage as the malformation, tying the AVM off at both sides eliminates circulation, causing the AVM, in the best of cases, to wither away. In many cases, where surgery has the potential for causing more damage than good, medication and close supervision are the only options.

The brain, and circulatory system that feeds it, like any good plumbing system, is pressurized. Fixing the leak in one place can put additional pressure on other weak areas, causing other leaks. "Plugging" an AVM occasionally results in bleeding elsewhere, a very dangerous side effect to tying-off.

In my case, not only was the rupture near the surface, a very good thing, it was in a part of the brain that was essentially dead. They could remove the malformation and surrounding tissue without major impact to brain function. My brain, over the forty-nine years I had been alive, had already adapted a work-around for the dead area. Miracle number six.

When I was first stricken, as the brain was shutting down, I became very ill. Violent vomiting and coughing, possibly a side effect of the bleeding brain, collapsed a lung. Lungs are more like a sponge than a balloon. Doctors inserted a tube to remove pressure from the lung cavity to allow the lung to reattach itself and refill with air. That tube would play a part in my later bad behavior.

They removed the part of the brain containing the malformation (it was essentially dead anyway) and cauterized the wound. I claim they used an ice cream scoop. I like ice cream very much even though the thought of a brain cone isn't very appetizing. I was under close observation. They did follow-up CAT scans to assure there was no additional bleeding. They wheeled me into the Intensive Care Unit (ICU) where Steve, my brother, sister, daughter and son awaited.

As proof that good things can and do happen, even in the face of calamity, a good friend gave us a cute little Bengal kitten. Rocky, the kitten, was born on the day of my surgery, the day of my Re-

Birthday. Bengals are very cute, often referred to as lap leopards. Bengals were originally crossbred from Asian leopards and domestic cats. He is going to be a big cat, but still cat-sized. He is precious and has rapidly become part of our family.

Rocky's nickname is Doodle because he is always doodling around. Rocky has simple rules. If it's edible it's food and if it isn't food it's a toy. Everything must be explored and enjoyed. Not a bad example for us humans. Maybe we should all be a bit of a Doodle.

Speaking of cats, Steve tells me I was Bad Kitty in the hospital, a pet name he uses for me when I'm doing something I shouldn't. I wouldn't leave things alone and kept trying to take off stuff attached to my body. They had to restrain me to prevent injury. I hate restraints and can't stand things covering my face. In my defense, I watched my father slowly pass while attached to all those things, so I learned to hate them.

Speaking of my Dad . . . I SAW HIM. At some point during my hospital stay he reached out to me. I can't prove when that happened, whether it was a dream or something more unexplainable. I can only tell you how I felt and what I believe.

He looked the way I want to picture him. He was in his late fifties or early sixties. Gone were the ravages of long term illness that I witnessed prior to his death. Thick auburn hair replaced thinning grey. His skin was glowingly healthy. His always thin body looked stronger and more durable. He flashed his award-winning smile.

I was immediately comforted. I knew instantly that all the theory about life after death would now be fact for me. There would no longer be doubt.

He reached his hand out to me, not as an invitation to join him, but more as an attempt to lovingly touch my shoulder. He told me that everything was going to be okay. I could not see my own body, but reached out to hug him anyway. When I did, he was gone, but the feeling inside me was not. Everything WAS going to be okay.

According to research on the subject, survivors of near death experiences generally fall into one of two categories. They either see a bright white light or they see a departed loved one telling them everything is fine. Both experiences seem to have a calming, reassuring affect on the nearly departed. Unless we are all victims of mass hypnosis, it is an often enough recurring marvel that it becomes difficult to dismiss it as mere reverie.

For those who scorn the possibility of afterlife, it was just a nice dream. For those who believe, it is easy to accept the phenomena as proof of passage to a safer, friendlier place.

It was real beyond mere unconscious vision. I know what dreams feel like and how I remember them when I am awake. This was different. I believe I saw my Dad, and I feel confident that, when I die, I will be going to a place filled with lost loved ones. I no longer fear death, but very much want to live long enough to tell as many people as I can that there is peace and existence at the end of the road.

Unfortunately, insightful experience or not, none of that made me a better patient.

I was clever, even though I don't remember it. I wanted the oxygen mask off my face, so I asked the nurse to raise the bed to a sitting position. When upright, I leaned forward and, even with my hands restrained, grasped the mask in one hand tightly enough to rip it off.

In so doing I also tore off the ventilation tube on top of my head. This was the medical device equalizing pressure on my brain, reducing the swelling. After a little brain fluid spilled, the nurses and doctors patched me back up and I was thereafter restrained even closer. Had a nurse not been right there when it happened, I would have been in terrible trouble. Miracle number seven.

Life is a Beach – Kat Sanders

Did I mention the chest tube for my collapsed lung? I ripped that out too. I now have a nice scar on my right side where the tube used to be. I was a bad patient. I really was Bad Kitty, even though I don't remember it.

I want to thank the medical staff, nurses and assistants. They were all very kind and considerate. At least that is what Steve says. One of the nurses was also a licensed manicurist. He apologized when he had to remove my beautiful fingernail adornments.

Polish was blocking readings from instruments attached to two of my fingers and had to go. He sympathetically removed the polish from all my nails so they would match, then buffed them so beautifully that I had to think twice about re-polishing them when I got home. They were so pretty.

I think his name was Chris. He, along with my sister, also helped clean and comb out my hair so I wouldn't lose it. Hair loss is common in surgeries such as this.

Many health professionals focus strictly on their discipline, ignoring the person as a whole. A quick message here to those entering or desiring entry to the medical profession. You are treating a PERSON not a malady. To the extent possible consider what might be important to the PERSON when making decisions. Mental outlook plays a very important role in recovery.

Loss of hair or ugliness of nails would mean little to Steve who, I think, occasionally combs his hair with an eggbeater. But to me they were very important. I looked bad enough coming out of surgery. I needed all the feminine attributes that could possibly be saved to feel better about myself. Thanks to hospital staff at Riverside Regional Medical, Steve and my sister, Cher, for feeling the same way. I appreciate every strand of hair I have. Thanks to my brother for telling me I'm pretty even when I know he is lying.

Steve said there was a point, on the second day after surgery, when he really worried about my recovery. Overnight readings were not good. Blood pressure, oxygen levels and heartbeat were not normal. Medical staff resorted to overnight medicinal controls.

The next morning I apparently woke up, opened my eyes and didn't recognize either him or our daughter. The day before, I had told the doctor who my sister, brother and husband were and called them all by name. I was reminding them about the appointments I had with clients. This time there was nothing.

All I wanted to do was sleep, common for brain trauma patients but also a possible indication of impending coma. When the brain is injured it wants rest, and coma is the ultimate rest. The morphine they were giving me for pain didn't help wakefulness either. Awareness became more important since awareness was necessary for taking a swallow test.

Swallowing is a very complicated voluntary response and an indication of the patient's eventual self-sufficiency. I was not awake enough to pass the swallow test, which meant I could not have solid food.

The day prior I had been more lucid and could have passed the test, but when my nurse asked me my name, I responded, "Kat."

She took this to mean that I thought I was a cat, and told the doctor as much. It wasn't till the following day, the day I was really out of it, that the nurse told Steve the story, to which he responded, "That is correct. Kat is her name."

"But she is not a cat," argued the nurse.

"That is her nickname," Steve responded, "It is short for Kathleen." to which the nurse sheepishly mumbled something about misinforming the doctor.

The delay was not as costly as it might have been. That day I was pretty incoherent anyway. Steve told Cher that the two of them needed to do something to motivate me out of the desire to sleep. Since I had not been fed for almost five days, hospital staff decided to put a feeding tube through my nose. When staff disclosed their intentions to Steve, he turned to Cher and said, "That will do it."

Sure enough, when they inserted the feeding tube I was instantly awake and fighting. Did I mention that I hate tubes? I apparently immediately complained about lizards crawling all over me and tried to take off my gown. Hallucinations induced by Morphine, are common. I eventually lost the lizards, opened my eyes and asked, "Why are you doing this to me?"

The nurse responded, "You haven't had food for a few days and you need nourishment so the brain can heal."

"Then get me a straw and some Ensure," I replied, to the relief of Cher and Steve.

I was back. After that, the only questions were how much of my former self would be lost and how much would immediately return. Each day got better. I passed the swallow test the following day and started on real food, presuming you can call hospital food real food. I didn't eat much, but ate enough to keep the nurses and doctors happy.

Steve was playing music in ICU to drown out code blues (emergency responses when someone stops breathing) and the sound of the automatic door opening and closing. One of my nurses was a concert fiend and commented on which of the acts she had seen or not seen. She asked Cher if she knew about the upcoming Heart concert near San Diego.

Heart is one of my all time faves. Steve and I had seen a sign on Interstate 15 advertising the concert and made a mental note to check it out. As usual, business got in the way and we forgot. When I heard the nurse talking, I opened my eyes and said "Get me a glass of milk and Heart tickets."

Needless to say one of the first things we did when we got home was order Heart tickets. It was a very cool concert and I rocked out from my wheelchair. The Wilson sisters sounded just as good as they had always sounded. Amazing.

There was one other musical note to my stay. My favorite male singer is Josh Groban. Whenever I struggled or seemed in stress, Steve would put Josh Groban on the Ipod player and I would immediately settle down, sometimes even sleep. It was almost like having Groban tuck me in. Odd but true.

Though I will swear to everyone who will listen that the positive thoughts and encouraging talk helped my recovery, I remember only one thing about my hospital stay. On the day I was to be released, they wanted to do one last CAT scan. I was afraid, believing the scan to be the same as an MRI.

I am highly claustrophobic. MRI's are a huge coffin-like tube.

If anyone puts me into a coffin, I promise to haunt them. Steve has instructions to give away my organs and burn me up, but never put me underground in confined space. I know I will be dead and won't care, but it gives me piece of mind, while I'm alive, that a coffin will not be my final resting place.

Sympathetic to my misplaced fear, the attendant, Michael, promised to hold my hand while they completed the procedure. Due to fears of radiation exposure, only medical staff is allowed into a CAT scan room. Steve could not be there, so Michael held my hand and comforted me. I don't even know Michael's last name, but this small and unnecessary thing he did was very important to me and consistent with how staff treated me at this hospital.

I do not like hospitals in general and was apparently anxious to get home. I say "apparently" because I still don't remember much of this time frame. They let me go home after a week and five days without extended outpatient physical, occupational or speech therapy. Miracle number eight.

When I got home, Steve had already set up our family room to be MY area. He even let me have control of the TV remotes. My computer was already on the coffee table (for my games and internet fun). The couch was mine, shared only with my cat, Nemo. Steve cooked, cleaned, helped me put my clothes on, helped me into and out of the bath.

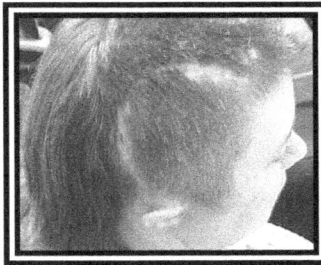

Kat's Craniotomy

Badge of Honor

My head was shaved on one side and the ugly scar was readily visible. I had wounds all over where tubes, IV's and other connections had been. I was not pretty. And, I was an emotional wreck. I am an impatient person by nature, but was even more impatient after the trauma. Though rational most of the time, I occasionally found myself in the middle of a crying bout and didn't know why.

In one of my low moments, I asked Steve why he still loved me and he said, "Because I love everything about you, and there is no one in the world like you."

I cried some more while he held me and realized that this was what true love was all about.

I knew it would take a year or more to get back to "normal". I was weak, unbalanced, and prone to moments of memory loss and emotion. Claustrophobia, normally quite manageable, became a really big deal.

I could remember a contract from a year ago, but couldn't remember the time, even if you told me five minutes ago. There was no way I could drive, and a real estate agent without wheels is as desirable as ants in ice cream.

Steve, bless his heart, picked up both the home and business load. While I rested, he worked. It gave both of us (but mostly me) time to think about priorities, which is how this book got started.

Did I tell you I was a Greenie? Oh yeah. I guess I did. Well one of the paper saving moves we made was to go completely electronic. Our ageents can get whatever they need through the internet, shared files and email. They are total road-warriors and never have to come into the office unless they choose to do so. PDF is good.

We set up our office so we can work wherever we happen to be. As long as we have our laptop we are connected. We can even print and sign checks while on a cruise ship. This served us well while I was in recovery.

Initially Steve had to be with me whatever I did, wherever I was. He helped me put on my underwear, picked out my clothes and made sure I took my medications. He was chauffer, cook, maid, business manager, slave to our pets (those of you with pets know what I mean), and communication center for family and friends. Most of this would not have been possible had we not set up our business they way we did. <u>Miracle number nine</u>.

We do not have doctorates, teaching credentials or ministry certifications behind our names. We have simply become more aware of what is important, not out of choice, but out of circumstance. We hope to pass that knowledge onto others, before it is too late for them to make changes.

I wrote this while still in recovery. I think it best describes the changes in direction and priority facing us after twenty years of marriage.

When I awoke on April 22nd, 2010 it was a day like any other day. Later that afternoon, while at home, my world changed forever. Suddenly, there was such a pain in my head – it felt like someone had stabbed me with a knife.

I called out to Steve. Before I could explain the extent of the pain, I lost my balance and fell to the ground. Once sitting on the floor, I had no ability to get back up. Why wasn't my body working? What was this pain in my head? Why was I so confused? I have little memory of the next two weeks beyond that moment.

After emergency surgery, I briefly remember waking up in the hospital with family and friends nearby. On their way to wish me well, none were sure I would survive. All came prepared to say their good-byes.

I survived, but must deal with how very close I came to death. I will struggle to regain my memory, my functions, my strength, but the alternative would have been much worse. What if I had died? There is so much I still want to say and do.

I was taken to the County facility where they bring gang members after a gang fight, killers, and felons wounded in gun battles with cops. It is where the indigent and unfortunate find themselves when there is no other alternative. Fortunately, both the facility and its medical staff were top notch, and they preformed what we now can say was a miracle. There were others in ICU with me who were less fortunate.

Through the medications and sleepiness following surgery, there were several code blues. A code blue is when someone is no longer breathing or their heart has stopped beating, requiring immediate medical attention. Steve, my brother and sister told me there were at least four or five while I was in ICU. Most of them did not make it.

Why was I given a second chance? What am I supposed to do with it?

I believe in the power of positive thinking and prayer, and I had hundreds of people praying for me. Regardless of your personal religious beliefs, the knowledge that hundreds of people care enough to think about you is inspirational. Positive thought as well as the knowledge that people care about you, aids in both survival and recovery. At very least it provides a reason to live, to fight through an experience like this.

So what do I do with my second chance? I have thought long and hard about this question, and have come up with a list of answers.

First, I've got to get my priorities in order. God, family and then work.

Life is short. Life is precious. Money isn't as important as it once seemed. Spending time with Steve, doing the things we've always wanted to do but always put off because of time or money (like that trip to Europe we've talked about for 20 years). Now is the time to revive those dreams and find a way to do them.

Then there's my son. He's all grown up, but he still needs me. My daughter, too. Though she is older and more secure, I need to tell her again how much I love and cherish her. There are things

I want to tell them both before I die...I almost didn't have that chance. Now I do and I'm not going to waste it.

Lastly, I want to make a positive difference in this world. I want my near-death experience to help others realize the preciousness of life and how in 5 minutes, it can be over. All of those things you want to say or do – do them now. Write your "bucket list" those things you want to do or accomplish before you die, and start checking them off one by one.

My new motto?

Live life to its fullest.

Enjoy the beauty of the world – its people, its uniqueness, its wildlife, its experiences. Sights, smells, sounds...they are all more "alive" than they were before...and I appreciate the chance to experience them.

Certainly, it's not all rosy. There are money issues. There are relationship issues. There are health challenges. Facing those issues and challenges with the knowledge that they are small things in the face of death, will help me overcome them, now that I have a second chance.

Even if you cannot change all that's wrong in your life, appreciate relationships more, or spend more time with the people who truly love you. You don't need a fancy house or an expensive car to hug your dog or feed the birds. Enjoy sunsets. Revel in the company of others. Embrace more, argue less.

We cannot control our destiny, or the day of our death. But, we can control how we react to the trivial that occurs in life. Like the Carlson's admonish in their book, "Don't Sweat the Small Stuff and it's All Small Stuff." We can get up, brush ourselves off and do the best we can with what we are given, or with what we have left.

I no longer fear death. I've been close enough to feel it. My faith assures me that there is a heaven. I am confident that family and friends await me. When I'm gone, I will join them, my Dad assured me of that, but I am going to make the best out of what's left of my life. I hope to convince family, those closest to me and strangers alike to embrace grace, kindness and love that allow us to live, happily and respectfully, perhaps celebrating together forever.

I know what you are thinking. I promised ten miracles and you only counted nine. Miracle number ten is the best and most important. Read on.

NOT the Rocky Doodle – Kat Sanders

CHAPTER TWO – Good & Bad Happen to Good People

Miracle 10

We discovered what is important in life. Miracle number ten is our primary reason for writing this book. Suddenly, complicated choices became crystal clear. I can tell you now what I am going to do with the rest of my life and it is a major change from where I thought I was headed. We started writing this book to remind ourselves about what we had learned and what it means to have a changed life.

Who is really in control?

We all want to believe that we are in control of our lives. We want to walk out the door each morning believing that we will reach our destination and return home safely. If we did not have that belief, we would all bury our heads under the pillow and never get out of bed. The belief that we are basically safe allows us to sit behind the steering wheel of a car, or board an airplane. It is as necessary as breathing.

Fortunately, that belief is not entirely accurate. We are all living out of control. None of us can assure, with any certainty, what may befall us on any given day. I say fortunately because many of the good things that happen are also totally off our radar screen.

Alexander Fleming was not thinking about his experiments when preparing for vacation. Hurriedly leaving a mess behind in his lab, he left on holiday. On his return, he discovered a strange culture in some of his experiments that bacteria seemed to avoid. On further study he discovered that this new concoction actually killed bacteria, thus Penicillin was invented.

Atlanta pharmacist John Pemberton was trying to find a cure for his personal morphine addiction. Like many wounded Civil War veterans, he had been treated with morphine. He threw a bunch of chemicals into water and, voila, Coke was created. Coke still keeps the original ingredients a closely guarded secret, so, outside Coca-Cola, no one actually knows what they were. Pemberton and his heirs made more money from soft drinks than from addiction medication, stomach or headache remedies.

3M chemist Spence Silver was trying to make glue. Instead he made a sticky substance that would only partially adhere to surfaces. He still thought there might be applications for glue that would not stick. 3M tried making a bulletin board that needed no thumbtacks, but that didn't sell. Art Fry, another 3M employee, looking for a way to get bookmarks to stick in his Hymnal, found a way to put Silvers glue to work. It worked so well that they circulated the sticky bookmarks to other 3M departments. Unfortunately, instead of getting new ones, employees were re-circulating the originals. How many bookmarks does anyone really need? One day Fry was looking for a way to add a note to one of his reports. He used one of the bookmarks, writing his comments on it. His colleague removed and pasted the sticky note on another report, along with his own hand written scrawl, returning it to Fry, and the Post It was born.

While few of us can create opportunity, we should all be ready to throw ourselves in its path. Those adamantly attempting to control their lives often miss opportunity while tunnel-blindedly (I made that up) trying to follow their own self-prescribed path.

Similarly, unreasonable refusal to risk pain eliminates the possibilities that come with such risk. Those of you who have fallen in love, only to be disappointed, will know what I'm saying.

Avoiding relationships, the alternative, delivers eventual loneliness or pain that is far worse. Forestalling pain cannot absolutely remove the possibility of calamity. Too many bad things are still completely out of our control.

Minding the Tide – Kat Sanders

According to the Center for Disease Control (CDC) about 616,000 people per year die from heart related illness. While many may be aware of their condition, many more are not, and even those who are aware probably would be hard pressed to predict the exact date of their death. Approximately 240,827 die from the flu, diabetes, and accidents in the home. Some 559,000 die from cancer. Almost 35,000 die every year from traffic accidents. Nearly 134,000 per year die from disease similar to mine, and most have no idea it is coming. Heck, some 90 people per year die from lightening strikes.

For the most part, none of these people were in control of their own fatality. How can we reasonably assume that each of us has enough control over our lives to predict what will or will not happen to us? Besides, we can learn from or experience benefits from both the good and bad that is out of our control. Few women would choose the pain of childbirth voluntarily, but look at the joyous end result.

Ironically, though we are in control of very little, we blame ourselves for everything. In point of fact, most of our life is out of our control and in the hands of someone or something else. Why not change our behavior, if ever so slightly, to accommodate the belief that something extraordinary, bad or good, could happen.

Consider the story of Jonah and the Whale. It starts with Jonah doing something he was told not to do. The bad boy boards a ship full of questionable characters. The ship ends up in the middle of a raging tempest. After Jonah asks for heavenly intervention, praying to be spared, the crew throws him overboard. Treading water, Jonah is on his way to meet Davy Jones.

Miraculously a big fish, some say a whale, jets toward Jonah and swallows him whole, saving him from drowning. Instead of digesting him, the fish spits Jonah out on shore, and, after a bit of personal reflection, Jonah ends up going where he was supposed to go in the first place.

There are several points to this story. For purposes of this book we are going to focus on one. Jonah certainly must have believed, at some point, that he was done for. He wasn't. He wanted to go one place and ended up in another. When the fish swallowed him he must have believed it was all over. Instead the fish delivered him back on shore, safe from the ravages of the storm.

It is not unreasonable to assume that all of this was unexpected. Jonah didn't board the ship with the intention of being brought back to shore by a fish. Even if this is merely a fable with no basis in reality, it brings home the point that we cannot predict what will happen next and we have little control over the ultimate result.

Steve and I are ordinary people. Until my hospital experience, we fought like all married couples fight. We said words we now know to be fruitless and harmful. We did not treat ourselves, each other, friends or family as well as we should. Our vision is now much clearer.

Our experience brought us closer and made us realize what priorities should be. We are writing this book to clarify for ourselves, and hopefully for others, what we learned.

Life is not, nor was it ever intended to be fair. We realize that we have to accept the good with the bad.

How can we consistently recognize the difference? I am never going to give up complete control, even when I know that control can cause anxiety. When should I exercise control and when should I submit. I need enough control to be balanced and confident, but not so much that it causes harm to me or others.

If determination of what is important and what is not becomes the basis for living a full life, for finding balance, for retaining happiness and contentment, how, exactly, do we do that?

Why Do Bad Things Happen to Good People?

I'm going to cover this briefly. It is a book unto itself and I don't want to steal thunder from those who have done a great job of writing about this before. If you need greater understanding, grab *When Bad Things Happen to Good People*, by Harold S. Kushner. His take is similar but far more in depth.

What happened to me was scary, uncomfortable and unfair and I am sure as I am alive, that it is not God's fault.

I am not really yet clear about what the answer is. I'm better at asking questions, but I do know that the God I know wouldn't do anything to harm me, even if he thought I would learn a lesson through it. He wouldn't cause me harm just to teach others. I can't speak for Nature, as nature leans towards chaos, but He loves me more than that.

We went to a great church in Vancouver Washington. The senior pastor, Matt Hannan, was an avid hunter, much to the dismay of many Bambi-loving members of his flock. He once made a comment that stuck with me.

"Though I've done a lot of duck hunting," he once quipped. "I've never shot a duck. I shoot in front of them and they fly into the bullets."

That is how life really is. Life is shooting at us all the time. Sometimes we fly into the bullets, other times we dodge them. There is nothing making us fly into the bullets. We could choose to fly elsewhere or in a different pattern and avoid them altogether, but if we are struck, it is not because God wants it that way. He is there to pick us up, dust us off, help us fix what is wounded and move on. But he is not firing the gun. At least that is how I see it.

While we are talking about bad things that happen to good people, can we take a moment to thank bunches of unsung heroes. There are more hidden casualties of bad things than victims. The family and loved ones are affected at least as much, and sometimes, are harmed more than those suffering the injury. Some have to abandon dreams or jobs in order to care for invalid family members. Some struggle to make ends meet due to oppressing medical bills or sudden loss of income.

Few of us think about them or think to help them. Sometimes they are so overwhelmed with surviving, or helping someone else survive, that they fall victims themselves. Sometimes they even have enough strength to pull it off, but it will never be without sacrifice.

Steve had to pick up all the responsibilities for our business, our pets, our home life, the bills, the cooking, the cleaning, the financial aftermath of income loss, and hospital bills. He had to chauffer me anywhere I needed to go and take me back when I was done.

He had to deal with butt-headed collectors, who often called six times a day, even when they knew we had no money and had been told about our medical problems. He had to handle our bankruptcy and foreclosure, a very tough thing for a proud, moral man.

Without him, I doubt you would be reading this. He supported the concept of this book and was my ghost in its writing and perceptions. He has done a miraculous job of keeping my spirits up and helping me to understand why all this happened.

Help those who need help by volunteering food or doing chores. In our case, there was lots of stuff that needed doing. Our business partners and employees picked up the ball and ran, without being asked. That's what it takes. Steve, like the family of many victims, was so overwhelmed by my injury and recovery that he didn't have the time to decide what it was he needed.

Between those who helped, those who prayed and power beyond mine, our business survived and so did I. I cannot prove that God was there, that's a matter of faith, but I know He was with me every step of the way. Steve, God, good medicine, our family and friends pulled me through.

God was with me through recovery, otherwise I would not be where I am. I also know that hundreds, if not thousands of people prayed for me, becoming my second family and spiritual pals. There is power in prayer and positive attention.

Many people learned lessons and changed direction in their lives because of what happened to me, proving that God can use calamity to help us without causing the calamity Himself. You don't have to be holding the smoking gun to treat the victim of a crime.

On faith you must decide for yourself why bad things happen to good people, because there are precious few facts to unequivocally prove anyone's belief. Faith is belief without proof.

I think I have the answer, but then, I had brain surgery. What do I know? Woo hoo!

Elephant Seal Bull -

Speaks His Piece - Kat Sanders

CHAPTER THREE – What's Important?

What is right for my life?

The greatest challenge facing most of us is deciding what makes us happy, then sticking to it. What we think makes us happy, in the short run, may not make us happy for life. What seems trivial today may be what we remember forever. We will discuss how to prioritize what we do in a later chapter. Let us first talk about what is important.

Our son, on a phone conversation, once asked "Am I a good man? Are you proud of me?"

As a good parent should, I responded immediately and without hesitation, "Of course!"

The answer was accurate, reinforcing and quick. He is in the Air Force, striving to better himself. He has more compassion than either anger or ego because he cares more for others than he cares for himself. He is more likely to be sucker for a sob story than become a famous, and would give you the shirt off his back. That is what makes him who he is. He is a strong, wonderful young man and I'm proud to be his mother.

Then I remembered our experience Steve once described in his blog.

My wife, son and I were bouncing along wind roughened waters in a rented power boat on Lake Pleasant near Phoenix. We don't get to see our son as often as we like, as he lives hundreds of miles from home. We rented the boat to have a memorable day, even though the wind was whipping and the water was full of whitecaps. The day would become more memorable than we could possibly imagine.

We noticed a boat floating near shore. We were still hundreds of yards away, but could see the people inside the boat anxiously waving a red flag, normally a warning to other boaters that a water skier is down. They were confused and didn't seem to know how to restart their stalled vessel.

Even at that distance we could see they were frantic. The water was too rough and cold for casual skiers and the boat was too near hidden sand bars for experienced boaters. I pointed our bow toward the becalmed boat and shoved the throttle forward.

As we neared, we could see two men in the water approximately 25 yards from their boat. Both were obviously tired and scared, drifting further and further from their craft. The looks on their faces told us everything we needed to know. They were in serious trouble. The better swimmer of the two was trying to hold the other man's head above water, but he was running on empty. Neither man was wearing safety equipment.

My son, Matt, grabbed two life vests and jumped overboard, delivering life saving equipment to the desperate pair. The man in greatest danger was barely able to hold onto the vest in the frigid water, but hold on he did. We swung the boat around, killed the engine so the propeller would not harm either my son or the men in the water. Matt climbed back into the boat and pulled both of them aboard.

We took them back to their boat, where they safely re-boarded. We shook their hands and left, never knowing who they were or how it all got started. They fired up their engine and made it back to shore. They never even got our son's name and wouldn't know how to thankfully contact him, but in our hearts, we knew that someone's brother or father or son was going to live beyond that day. Shivering all the way back to the docks, that knowledge was Matt's only reward.

No one else saw what Matt did. There were no bands playing or mayors offering keys to the city, nor were any of those a thought in his mind when he jumped into icy water to save two men on the verge of drowning. No one, outside those who read this story, will fathom his desire to help or save others. And he did it without thought for his own safety, without wondering whether or not it was worth his time or effort. He did it with the sole intent of helping someone else. That is what makes a good man.

Like the rest of us, he's made mistakes, but that is not the measure of a man. We all make mistakes. The true measure of human worth is what we do when no one is looking. When surrounded by peers or police, we all toe the line. What we do when only God can see makes us who we really are.

Matt, much to his mother's chagrin, likes motorcycles and spends much of his spare time alternately riding and fixing them. Age and experience will teach him that no one, including him, will remember how fast he rode or how high he jumped, but there are two men, two families, who will never forget him, even if they don't know his name.

Matt's experience should have made him happy. It certainly made the two men he saved and their families happy. But he didn't see it as any big deal. He assured us that anyone in the same circumstance would have done the same thing. Even after Steve instructed him that many people would have driven their boat by, in fact many did, Matt still didn't grasp the importance of what he had done.

Matt is not alone. Most of what we do seems trivial, unnoticed, even insignificant in the scheme of things. We tend to exaggerate the stuff in our life that is meaningless and forgo celebrating events that make the world and our lives better. Why is that, and how can we turn that around to bolster contentment? That is our challenge.

Fame and fortune are often mistaken for validations of self worth. But, there are poor, unheralded men and women the world over who are more valuable to society than any Hollywood millionaire. Human worth is based on sacrifice, willingness to do what is right, regardless of cost or personal benefit, and the knowledge that even when we do the right thing, no one may notice.

Winning brings temporary fulfillment, but victory engenders losers as well as winners. Power enhances some at the expense of others. Ego, by definition, can only be self-gratifying. What, then, brings happiness?

Understanding the difference between what can and cannot be changed, discovering what is right instead of focusing on who is right, brings greater joy. Life is compromise and acceptance. Living with the foibles and differences of others is tough, and can result in outward disagreement, but acceptance of others is a necessary component of happiness.

Be nicer to each other. Even the smallest kindness or forgiveness triggers love, compassion and thankfulness. All good. Attitudes transcending self produce better outcomes than wallowing in the muck of ME, ME, ME.

What kind of attitude returns as much as it gives? What makes us happy? If, like most folks, you are still have trouble figuring it out, read on.

What makes us Happy?

There have been countless studies on what makes us happy or unhappy. Many have refined their findings to simple charts or analytic descriptions.

For Example, the Maslow chart is often used as a point of reference and discussion and is most likely the best empirical description of what makes life worthwhile.

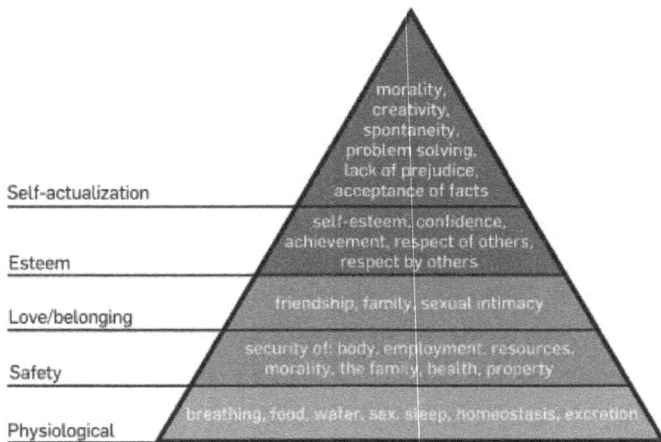

Maslow describes areas of both meaning and survival in his analysis. The individual's level of achievement in any of these areas defines both physical well being and how we feel about ourselves. That, in turn, defines how happy we are or are not.

Though one may argue the placement of the various elements in the chart, this is possibly the best analytic analysis of happiness and we would certainly not disagree.

Corona Del Mar Crane – Kat Sanders

For those without a doctorate in psychology, we have a much simpler approach.

SMALL

Safety

Morality, forgiveness, grace, respect and manners

Achievement, legacy and satisfaction

Love, subservience, sacrifice and spirituality

Learning and knowledge

When we make ourselves small, putting others or mankind ahead of personal endeavor, we grow much larger and become much happier. As self-centered children we always wanted to be on the receiving end of birthday presents, but as we grow more mature, we relish giving the correct gift even more.

The misunderstanding that we should be bigger than life, with power or control over our lives or others, cannot be true. As we discussed before, there is far too much in our lives over which we have no control. This belief in power causes us to stumble and the attempt to achieve power is eventually doomed to failure and frustration. For example, you cannot make someone love you.

Absolute power over others or our environs cannot be achieved by any man. Those historically attempting such power (Caesar, Napoleon, Alexander the Great, Genghis Khan, Hitler) have repeatedly proven as much. Learn from their mistakes. Power comes from within, from the basic understanding that controlling others or the universe is not possible.

While necessary for prodding ourselves to achieve, ego gets in the way more often than it helps.

BIGGER IS NOT BETTER. SMALL MAKES US TALL

When we inflate who we think we should be, as we create goals doomed to fail, after we strive for the material and do not achieve, we feel bad. If we think small, stay small and are satisfied with small, we become more happy and content.

This is not to say that we should not set goals for ourselves and attempt to achieve. Moral goals, spiritual goals, family goals are not measured by the pound or dollar. They are measured in smiles and memories. They are inexpensive to achieve and priceless in the end.

It is the belief that we are all due a castle and coffers of cash that keep us from happiness. Nearly every religious and moral philosopher points to the fruitlessness of material pursuit. If our reward is strictly pecuniary, happiness will be temporary and satisfaction will remain elusive.

Pain, poverty, persecution, abuse, bigotry, anger, perversion, slavery and ignorance are all part of the physical world. Those willing to advance at the expense of others WILL be more powerful and more monetarily successful, or they will end up in jail. They will relish temporary victory, but they cannot be content in the end.

Spirituality, achievement, appreciation and love are rewards worthy of pursuit. Leaving a legacy, not measured in gold, makes us a personal success.

SAFETY – Basic Human Needs

What do humans need to survive?

> Food
>
> Water
>
> Clothing (most of us have little fur, if any)
>
> Shelter

People without any of the above four will not feel whole or safe. Fear of losing, or absence of any of the above, are the basis for discontentment, illness or worse. There are many other things we may lack, but we will survive if we have all of the above, even if we are not happy.

Food

While we can argue the health benefits of eating properly or eating things with faces, no one will argue that without food altogether, we will not survive. Everyone needs basic sustenance.

"No man can worship God or love his neighbor on an empty stomach," quipped Woodrow Wilson.

Fasting in observance of religious rituals to the contrary, Wilson's point has validity. Fasting is a temporary, self-induced pain, where starvation is not. An empty stomach can prevent thought or prevail over it. The need for food will take a higher priority than the search for truth, morality, or even basic human kindness. Belief that the next meal will arrive allows us to carry on and thrive. Worry that a meal is days or more away, if at all, makes life miserable.

We can also let food become too high a priority by eating too much or wanting to eat too much. We can allow food, like a drug, to become an obsession or drug to replace love, friends, or absence of worth. Food should be used for the purpose intended, fuel for the body. If used for any other purpose, food will make you unhappy.

An exception can be made for those who appreciate haut cuisine. For them, food is a joyful hobby, but only as long as the epicurean delight does not compromise health.

Continued happiness requires a full stomach.

Water

In this country, we take water for granted. We shouldn't, but we do. There are droughts and we still water the lawn more often than is needed and wash the car. We leave the hose running or the faucet on. We spurn water resistant plants in favor of more tropical and water intensive growth. Even when we install hardscape we wash it down instead of using a broom.

In Third World countries, water is a precious commodity, more valuable even than diamonds. Without water, crops, livestock, even basic human health are not possible. Where people drink from tainted wells or brown puddles, illness and death surely follow.

Years ago Steve and I travelled to Honduras where sewers consisted of curbs and gutters. Rain washed human and animal waste into the drinking water system. According to our twelve-year-old guide, when the tides rose, good water came in to take the bad water out. But, the system would never work properly. It wasn't designed to remove all the waste or sediment that would leach into ground water and wells. Obviously, we didn't drink the water.

The Hondurans were better off than much of the world. At least they had water.

Lest we mistakenly believe that this only pertains to Third World countries, the city of Los Angeles was built on the power and influence of water rights. There was intrigue, murder and theft. For an entertaining history lesson, rent the movie Chinatown (Jack Nicholson-Faye Dunaway). It was all about the water.

Thirst is worst. Clean water is needed for health and contentment. Dirty water cannot create happiness.

Clothing

Unless you are a polar bear, with lots of natural fur to protect you from the elements, clothing and footwear are required to protect us from sharp objects, cold weather and the sun's scorching rays.

The concept of need is difficult to define. Had clothing been topic for discussion of need several generations ago, there was a need for a dress, gloves and shoes for women, perhaps a hat, and a suit, shirt and shoes, perhaps a hat, for men. Functional undergarments were also required.

In today's world, there is NEED for a formal outfit (church, special occasions) though less so than in previous generations. We should all have a business uniform, whether a pantsuit, three piece vested suit, blouse, dress, shirt and tie (though again, not often as necessary as before). We need undergarments that enhance and protect. We need leisure clothes for fun and activity and shoes that go with all the above.

Even the poorest of the poor have gone fashionista, with appropriate logos, whether legitimate or counterfeit. If it fits, it protects us from exposure and is reasonably clean, it is all we NEED. Yet, we want the most current fashion and are unsatisfied if the people at work or kids at school think we are not cool.

Particularly for those in the tweens, teens and twenties, style statement seems necessary. Watch TV ads and decide for yourself who is buying. It isn't the older folks they're talking to. As we grow older, we are more concerned about comfort and utility. Perhaps we should all grow older quicker, then there would not be a need for fashion statements.

Presuming that we are not going to turn sixty at sixteen, what is a more logical solution. Joining a convent or moving in with Quakers is probably not in the cards for most of us. But, if on a limited budget, we could buy something fashionable strictly for those special occasions, whether or not others have seen us in it before. That might solve the problem.

Steve had to wear pink jeans to high school. He went through the beach craze. White jeans and pants were hip. His white pants got washed with a red shirt. He then had pink. His family could not afford new pants, so he wore pink.

He worked weekends to make enough money to buy a pair of cool slacks (that were not pink). He discovered that wearing one cool outfit a few times a week, though repetitive, made him okay if not cool. This may not work today, but it was a reasonable compromise then.

Wouldn't it be better if we all compromised a little bit? And wouldn't it be better still if we went out of our way to accept and compliment the fashion challenged, particularly those who cannot afford the luxury of fancy clothes? (See Morality, forgiveness, appreciation and manners later).

Without shirt and shoes the only place one can be happy is on a warm sandy beach.

Shelter

There are indigent people the world over that would love a roof, or even cardboard box, over their head. Homeless families, living in our cities and suburbs, would thank their lucky stars for a night's stay out of the cold and dank.

How receptive to happiness would you be if you had to share your living space with rats or roaches or street gangs? How comfortable would you be if mold and mildew permeated the walls of your abode? How good would you feel if your home was a cardboard box? This is an area in which we can all do better in helping others get shelter (see Achievement, legacy and satisfaction below).

A clean, safe place in which we can shelter our food, water, clothing and ourselves is critical to continued happiness.

Getting Involved

I happen to be a political conservative, but must also full-heartedly acknowledge liberal concerns. If we hope to reduce the size of government, then private citizens and business must do a better job of providing safety nets. If you don't volunteer time or donate to non-profits, if you don't help out with church sponsored soup kitchens, if you are too busy to coach or mentor kids, you proliferate the problem. If you don't get involved, you leave the job to government and have no room to criticize.

More importantly, giving back is one of the best ways to feel good about yourself, thereby achieving happiness. Helping other people be happy makes us happy. We will discuss this in length later, but imagine how good you could feel by taking on even one of the above causes.

Now that the basic needs have been covered, let's move onto more esoteric, but no less important, ingredients of happiness.

What Makes YOU Happy?

One last variable to consider in your search for happiness. What is it that winds your clock? What are the important things in life TO YOU?

Each of us is different. Each of us has personal desires, likes, dislikes, dreams, fantasies, and goals. How do you identify those things that make YOUR life worthwhile? Activities later in this book will help you single out what is important to YOU, but first lets talk about what makes most people feel good.

Can You See Me? - I'm hiding and really **SMALL**

CHAPTER FOUR – Morality Matters

Morality, forgiveness, respect and manners

In the movie "Duets", one of the lead characters quips "Society has lost its finesse."

This is my favorite movie quote. To many of us in mid-life, the statement seems abundantly true. Manners, class, appreciation, morality, honesty, forgiveness and basic human kindness seem as endangered as the dodo bird.

Watch any of the reality shows and you can see for yourself what some people are thinking. Participants on these shows are underhanded, driven to do whatever it takes regardless of the importance, or lack thereof, of the eventual goal. They are often just plain mean to each other.

Is winning at any cost the new trend? What if the price we pay for victory demeans who we are? What if winning is at the expense of someone weaker, in greater need, or more worthy than ourselves? Is that what life is really all about?

Even when winning IS important, some victories are worth more than others. We all know when we deserve the win. We also know when we steal it.

When your team has less talent, but your game plan proves better than theirs, those are victories worthy of celebration. If winning means cheating or bending rules or unnecessarily hurting others, how can that be good? Unjust wins prove nothing and mean nothing.

Athletes deserving of admiration are those who point heavenward, or to their teammates or coaches, or who run into the stands to hug their loved ones. Those who merely fist pump or chest thump miss the point. It is never about ME. It is always about US. Good sportsmanship and teamwork will never go out of style.

True Winners

Sara Tucholsky of Western Oregon University took a mighty cut and lofted her first high school/college homerun over the centerfield fence. She was a senior and it was likely that it would be her last home run as well. She was not a power hitter.

As she rounded first, she realized in her glee that she missed the base. She stopped and turned to tag the bag, so she would not be called out. A sharp pain in her knee brought her to the ground. She crawled back to first, but could not finish the victory trot around the bases.

Her coach called time out. The umpire said that she would have to either make it around all the bases or she would be officially given a single, disqualifying Sara's one and only home run. By rule, if any of Tucholsky's Teammates helped her, she would be called out.

To everyone's surprise, the opponent's first baseman, Mallory Holtman, asked the umpire if the opposing players could assist Tucholsky around the bases. The umpire said there was no rule against it. Holtman, homerun leader in the Great Northwest Athletic Conference, and her teammate, shortstop Liz Wallace, carried Tucholsky around the bases, allowing her to touch each base with her uninjured toe, before preceding to the next.

By the time they reached home plate the entire Western Oregon team was in tears, as were most of the spectators in the stands. It cost Central Washington the game and ended their chances of advancing to the playoffs. But, it was the right thing to do.

No one will remember who won the tournament or the conference. Few of us will ever be devoted fans of Central Washington or Western Oregon, but few will forget the sportsmanship, camaraderie amongst competitors or just the good feeling that comes from doing what is right.

Wherever Holtman and Wallace are today, they should somehow be rewarded for their integrity. Central Washington coach Gary Frederick should have been Coach of the Year for teaching his players fair play. Wherever Fredrick is today, he will surely never forget that shining moment that all coaches aspire to inspire.

Parents of college hopefuls should want their kids on his team. He's doing something right.

Athletes play games with set rules and timeframes designed to create winners and losers. Games are part of life, but games are not life. Game winners are not necessarily winners in life. Winners in life do not always win games. A gracious loser is far more likely to have their values straight than an obnoxious winner.

Morality

What we do does matter. Despite Presidents arguing the definition of "is", morality has a consequence far beyond doing right. Where there is no morality there is chaos. If everyone defined fairness and equality through their own eyes, the world would be a far more unfair place than it already is.

There is right beyond personal definition. There are undeniable truths to which we and our governments must either aspire to or die miserably. Were that not true, why is there a Declaration of Independence *("We hold these truths to be self-evident . . .")* and why is there a preamble to our constitution *("We the People of the United States, in Order to form a more perfect Union, establish Justice, insure domestic Tranquility, provide for the common defense, promote the general Welfare, and secure the Blessings of Liberty to ourselves and our Posterity, do ordain and establish this Constitution for the United States of America.")*

Wealth attained through stealth and misdeeds bites back. Achievement by such means is fleeting and eventually unimportant. The friends we forsake, the decisions we make and business we take live beyond our time. If we do wrong, or wrong is done to us, the scales eventually return to balanced, and we have little power over the how, when or where.

There is a moral compass in most of us. When we stray from its direction, we both know it and suffer from the deviation. That is called conscience. Those without a moral compass are also without conscience. They have no respect for others nor do they care what others think. Paradoxically, they demand and will go to any length, even kill, to avoid being disrespected.

We can only be happy and feel good about who we are when we both have and follow that moral compass. Know what good is, do what is good and you will feel good. Do what you know is wrong and, well . . . you know the rest.

"There is nothing divine about morality; it is a purely human affair. If people are good only because they fear punishment, and hope for reward, then we are a sorry lot indeed. What the individual can do is to give a fine example, and to have the courage to uphold ethical values ... in a society of cynics," said Albert Einstein.

Einstein was a smart guy, far smarter than me, in fact, and is correct with one slight exception. Morality transcends the human condition. Morality, like the basic laws of physics that Einstein so aptly applied, is unwaveringly true at its core. The moral basics are "self evident."

Most religious philosophies try to groom brotherhood, respect, proper behavior and love, all moral basics. To the extent these moderate directions are followed, society regains a measure of finesse. But, when imbibing the teachings of radicals, people shoot themselves in the foot.

Robert Fulgham, author of *All I Really Need to Know I Learned in Kindergarten*, summed it up best. He describes fair play, cleanliness social interaction and the basic rules of life that most of us learned in our first year of school. The concepts of human interaction are that basic. It is perplexing that so many have strayed so far from such simple truths.

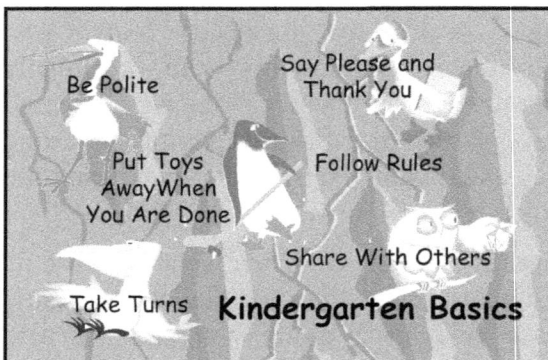

Kindergarten Basics: Be Polite · Say Please and Thank You · Put Toys Away When You Are Done · Follow Rules · Share With Others · Take Turns

Fulgham is a genius at making the

difficult understandable. Political sites, inspirational sites and guidance websites alike quote his work. If you have not read at least one of his books, you are missing out,

But I forgive you for that. Speaking of grace, how does that play into our desire for happiness? There is a chapter for that.

Kat and Steve Renew Their Wedding Vows – 20th Anniversary

CHAPTER FIVE – Forgiveness and Grace

Forgiveness

While morality is easy to understand and achieve when we are willing, forgiveness is the toughest human trait to develop. It should be the easiest, since all we have to do is forgive. Unfortunately, most of us would rather hang our hat on revenge or justice, which is why this is a chapter of its own.

Just a few words of advice. . .

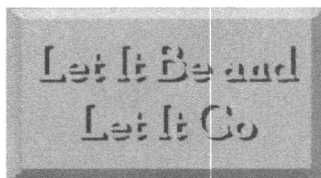

Let It Be and
Let It Go

John Lennon scribed:

Let it be, let it be, let it be, let it be.

Whisper words of wisdom, let it be.

We only hurt ourselves when we hold onto injuries, slights, insults, and wrongs done to us by others. Alternately, when our conscience prevails, we demean ourselves remembering the offenses we have committed. We should do what we can to affirmatively apologize, but need to stop beating ourselves up. It is not always within our power to correct past wrongs done by us or to us.

Justice is not within our personal control. Government has the monopoly on justice and justice is what any given court or government says it is. If one believes in a Supreme Being, justice probably resides in the hands of that ultimate power, who then uses man or society to exact required justice. Unfortunately, such justice could take decades or well beyond our lifetime to accomplish. At very least, the person doing wrong might have to wait for their own "judgment day" for justice to prevail.

"Vengeance is mine," sayeth the **LORD**.

Unless you are a Supreme Being yourself, vengeance and revenge are probably not in the cards either.

Nobody said that life is fair. People will do bad things to others and get away with it. While those committing crimes punishable by the state should be caught and brought to justice, those who wrong us in personal ways may never even know we have been hurt. Power to exact justice or revenge is rightfully curtailed by societal convention and our own sense of morality. We need to forgive and move on.

If someone cuts us off on the freeway, we don't pull out the Smith and Wesson and plug them. If someone's dog ruins our pansies, it is not acceptable for us to run over their dog. If someone angers us because they said or did something objectionable, our anger back for the perceived misdeed, even when justified, hurts only us.

There was a young woman whose life was harmed when she was sexually abused by her stepfather. For many years she carried the memory of the dark deeds with her and made poor choices in life as a result of the original tragedy.

She finally found her life path when she forgave her then deceased stepfather for his transgressions. She carried his ghost on her shoulders for years longer than he lived. He, and the negative he represented, could only conclude a well-deserved death, if she forgave and let him go. Holding onto bad memories and anger keeps bad legacies alive.

Another story tells of a missionary in the Amazon who was crossing a steamy river. When he emerged from the brown water he was covered with leaches. His immediate response was to start pulling them off. Fortunately his guide stopped the missionary before he could remove even one.

The guide explained that pulling them off would leave pieces of the leach under his skin, causing infection. Instead the guide made the missionary take a balsam bath. When the leaches relaxed in the bath, they let go and were removed without harm to their host.

We must remember to act slowly, not quickly in our attempts to right perceived wrongs. Unfortunately, knee-jerk reactions to those who wrong us tend to be the rule. Our anger or attempt at revenge usually harms us more than the original wrong.

Besides, such wrongs may be unintended or cultural. I studied sociology in college (just a couple of years ago) and remember that some cultures need more space than others. Anglo culture, particularly in the western US, needs an arms length to be comfortable, where many other cultures need less than half that.

Should I be angry because someone gets too close and bumps into me or should I forgive, understanding the difference between our respective habits or cultures? They are not doing it to ME. People committing offenses are generally not doing it to us personally. That is just who they are and they may not even understand that they are causing harm. We must be ever vigilant that we don't interpret OUR sense of right and wrong as THE measure of right and wrong.

The world may not punish wrong doers, but it certainly lets them know they are doing wrong, so there is no excuse.

At the Portland, Oregon airport a man, hastily making his way down the crowded corridor, lowered his shoulder and literally lifted me a foot in the air and knocked me off my feet. Only a few short months out of brains surgery, the hard fall could have ruptured the cauterized repairs, killing me.

Of course he didn't know that, but he should have been more considerate. He never even looked back. He could have said "I'm sorry."

I have no idea what he was thinking and if I guess I might be wrong when presuming he is a jerk. It is possible that my assumption is correct but I might also be wrong.

What if he was about to miss a flight home to his dying wife, or he was a Secret Service agent running to protect the President? Would that change my perception of him. You bet. I don't know his motivation and by guessing, I'm painting a picture that may prove false.

The good news is that six or seven onlookers rushed to my aid. One lady, probably in her sixties, ran after the man, pointing a finger in his face, scolding him.

Looking at this incident in macro-vision, good people seem to outnumber bad ones six or seven to one. Pretty good odds and reason enough to be positive about the world we live in. Yes, bad things will happen, but good people are right there next to you willing to help.

One of the female onlookers touched my life forever. I was embarrassed, sitting on my behind in the midst of a crowded airport. She sat on the floor with me and held my hand so I wouldn't feel so alone and asked if I was okay.

At that moment she created a legacy, even though she didn't know it. She is memorialized in our book and in all of our seminars, even though I didn't get her name. I will remember her forever and it cost her maybe three minutes of her life.

Unfortunately, we also must recognize that not all wrongs will be righted. Attempts to right a wrong are good, but only if in so doing we are not equally wrong. If unable to correct a bad situation by doing good, abandon the effort. Otherwise, our attempts to correct may boomerang, making us look or feel even worse than we did before. Attempting to poison a wrongdoer's well, poisons us as well. In most cases, we are better off forgiving than seeking revenge.

Notice, I said FORGIVING . . . I didn't say forgetting. We should do what we can to put the wrong out of our minds. Festering ill will induces ulcers and ulcers are a bad thing. But, offering the other cheek so it too may be struck, strikes me as foolish.

If someone has "done you wrong," first talk about it with friends, family or, in the toughest of cases a counselor, to make sure that molehills are not becoming mountains in your personal telescope.

If, after discussing the issue with third party bystanders, all agree that you are at the top of a bad Mt Everest, do what you can to assure that the offense cannot be repeated. Turn the other cheek, but don't let them strike again.

If it is an abusive relationship, this may mean moving out, or relocating. Physical health and well-being are basic human rights. There is no excuse for abuse. Anyone habitually harming others should be scorned and avoided.

Report physical and sexual abuse to the proper authorities so bad behavior won't be repeated. That is not revenge. That is self-preservation. Even if authorities fail to act this time, it will prepare them for the next.

Failing to report abuse and illegal activity is not cool. Despite depictions in The Godfather, there is nothing good about thief's honor. Pretense that we should never "rat someone out" condones and enables bad behavior. If it is legally wrong, it needs to be either stopped or legalized. Until legal, it should be discovered and corrected.

Occasionally the wrongful deed is very small, a little thing that drives us crazy. What do we do when a parent lets their child behave badly, or someone cuts in front of us in line? Will suggesting or insisting on corrections cause more hard feelings than simply ignoring the anti-social act? Would attempting to correct such misbehavior make me feel better or worse, particularly if the offender doesn't see the need for change?

Sometimes ignoring the offense is the best course of action. Granted, it doesn't educate the offender. They may still believe they are doing the right thing, or they may not care. Either way, the chances of corrective action are not very likely. It is far more likely that my comments will further anger an already angry person, and that wouldn't feel very good, so what would be the purpose?

If I take time to look for the good in people around me, I find the world to be a much happier place. That well-behaved adorable child at the zoo in amazement at the animals, the polite young man that holds the door open for me, that nice lady that lets me in front of her in the grocery line because I only have a couple of items to purchase make life better.

Wouldn't it make sense to purposely do nice things for other people, making both you and them happier instead of focusing on petty wrongs? Two wrongs can never equal a right, but enough rights can make wrongs seem miniscule. Pay it forward, making you a happier person.

Grace

If you think Forgiveness is tough, grace is even tougher. Grace is forgiveness without the expectation of anything in return. If that sounds too Godly for humans, you are thinking in the right terms.

Sometimes we forgive with the expectation that the person receiving forgiveness will recognize our act of kindness and will somehow beg for atonement. We want them to admit something or acknowledge something, or look us in the eye with puppy dog eyes begging for forgiveness.

The following is a true story Steve wrote about Grace:

I dropped my wife off at the airport. She was going out of town for a training excursion. She took her car and house keys out of her purse, along with the attached pepper spray. She would be back the next day. It was a short trip. She didn't need these heavy items in her purse, so she stowed them in the car's glove box for the time being..

I attended a Quantum Leap seminar in Temecula, CA the following day. It is a two day class about priorities and goals and how to get there. It's a great class if you've never experienced it.

At the end of the day, I went straight from the seminar to the airport to pick up my wife Kat. I met her at baggage claim (she is seldom able to travel without real luggage), we hugged, made our way to the car and drove home.

The following morning I had to get up early to make it to Temecula on time for day two of the seminar. I had been on the road for about a half hour, and was making good time, when my cell phone rang.

"I'm sorry," said Kat on the other end. "I can't find my keys. Do you know where they are?"

Immediately the truth came to me. I opened the glove box, while doing my best to stay in my own lane, and there they were. I was angry that they would still be there. Both our fault really, but in the heat of passion, anger and blame reared their ugly head.

I wanted to rant about responsibility and vent the frustration I felt, because I knew I would have to turn my car around and head back home. She could do nothing without house keys, car keys and office keys, all on the key ring in my glove compartment.

Unfortunately I was a half hour from home. I would now be late for the seminar. Fortunately I was a half hour from home and had time to cool down.

When I arrived, Kat was waiting at the front door. She looked very sad. Thinking she was just feeling badly about taking me out of my way, I gave her a quick kiss on the cheek, handed her the keys and jumped into my car to head back down the road.

Ten minutes later, back on the freeway, my cell phone rang. It was Kat.

"My sister called just before you got back," she said, choking back tears. "My Mom has been diagnosed with terminal liver cancer."

A thousand possibilities flew through my head. I asked if she needed me to come home. She said no. She said there was nothing I could do and I would be back that afternoon anyway. I offered to come back anyway and she said she would prefer to have some time alone. I continued to the seminar, but my heart wasn't there.

What if I had been a jerk, not that out of character for me? How good would our relationship have been if I verbally blasted her when she was already depressed? That alone would have been good reason to question our relationship.

The lesson here? We never really know what others are thinking and can never quite be sure that everything is on an even keel. We are often one bad conversation away from critically injuring someone we love. We need to think before we speak, even when we believe ourselves to be justified. Right does not justify might if the effect is hurting someone we shouldn't.

I am so glad I kept my cool that morning and didn't show frustration. Kat was appreciative that I would come home to bring her the keys without making her feel any smaller than she already felt. Our relationship grew stronger through my lack of judgment and helped her through the shock of her bad news. Three short months of illness then the eventual passing of her mom were less traumatic because she trusted me to help her through it.

So I was late to my training class. I was not too late to show my wife how much I cared. Far more important. And as it turns out, really good timing for once.

Practice Grace, even when it hurts.

Rocky Doodle the Re-Birthday Kitten *– Kat Sanders*

CHAPTER SIX – Respect and Manners

Respect

Steve and I are not proponents of the everyone-should-be-in-first-place philosophy. We see the value in competition and a desire to achieve. Schools and programs that make everyone a winner, demean value, at the expense of those who truly achieve.

Sports in particular seem to be a target for academia, many of whom fear that competition is bad. If competition and the desire to achieve are bad, why then do these same people hypocritically support mathematical, literary, art, music, dance and academic competitions? Why are there grades?

As I've said before, sports are not life. They are games in which there are winners and losers. Advantage goes to the swift the strong, and the well-coached. Those at the peak of their game, just like those who sit first chair in the orchestra, must be acknowledged for their achievement.

Imagine how it would sound if the symphony allowed anyone carrying a violin to play. How good would Phantom of the Opera sound if untalented Karaoke singers were cast in lead roles? Would it be fair or right to allow some children to misspell words in a Spelling Bee just to make things more even? Poor grammar, misplaced modifiers and lack of punctuation would make for poor reading, should we condone and publish it anyway? Respect is a small price to pay for quality.

Respect extends beyond entertainment. Do we adequately appreciate those who have given their lives so we can live the lives we do; military, police, firemen, teachers, moms, dads, coaches and doctors? And what about the invisible people who make the world run; sanitary workers, contractors, maids and waiters.

A college professor once asked his students to list the ten most important jobs.

At the top of list were the usual suspects; doctors, teachers, firemen . . . The teacher then explained to the class that in the 1400's, while the plague was raging, doctors were less important than garbage men and porters who carried the dead away.

The Black Death (bubonic plague) took so many lives that just removing the bodies was more important than treating the ill. Doctors knew little about the malady, and the affluent wouldn't venture out of their homes, but grave diggers and morticians knew what to do.

There was a total breakdown of societal convention. Lawlessness and chaos reigned. It would have been far worse had the dead been left in the street.

The professor went on to explain that society is like the human body. Each organ, each tissue, each cell has a necessary function. Lacking all the right parts, the body, as a whole, can cease to function. Every job in society is worthy and necessary for the good of the whole. Were that not true, garbage and transportation strikes would never occur.

Respect for the disabilities and weaknesses of others should also be placed much higher on our list of priorities. At the time we wrote this, I could not yet handwrite well. Learning to write again is difficult. Shaking makes tough motor skills even tougher.

There is a waitress suffering from the same malady as I and is afraid that she will not be able to keep her job. She is not able to write orders well. What is wrong with people? Why should her job be in jeopardy simply because her penmanship is off? A little human kindness goes a long way. They should allow her to be slower and have poor handwriting if she can still perform all the other functions of being a waitress. How can we expect to keep our self-respect if we have so little respect for others.

A message to those who park in handicapped spots when they shouldn't, WE NEED THOSE SPOTS. For a few months after surgery I needed a wheelchair. I also needed handicap parking. In most retail locations there were none available. Often there were cars without proper plates or placards. Even for those cars properly marked, many of the drivers were obviously healthy.

My bet is that the placard or plate belonged to a family member. That does not legally or ethically give every driver of the car the right to use handicap parking.

While I'm on the subject, get out of the way of people with canes or wheelchairs. Those beating the handicapped just because they can, are certainly not doing what they could to inspire a better life. How can they feel good when bettering someone less able than themselves?

Instead, when you see someone struggling to walk or with an armful of packages, hold the door open for them. As we've said before, it will make you both feel better about the world. Respect and happiness are mutual. We all feel better when doing things for others.

Most of the time, we know when we have accomplished or done something worthy of accolade, whether or not anyone notices. Though positive reinforcement from others is nice, it isn't necessary. Our self-respect is built on what WE know is right, not on what someone else tells us or forces us to do.

Appreciate everyone you meet and treat them with the respect they deserve. You'll feel better about yourself and, in the long run, have a happier life.

Manners

To many, this sub-category may seem foolish. Aren't manners and respect the same thing? How will manners help us feel good or worthwhile? Nobody really cares how we eat, if we pass wind or belch in public. Au contraire.

Let's say that you spot someone in a wheelchair in front of you as you are entering the movie theater. You decide to:

a.   Walk more quickly so you can get in front of them. It takes so long for someone in a wheelchair to get through the door.

b.   Walk more slowly, creating space between you and them so you won't have to wait as long.

c.   Hold the door open for them so they can more easily get through.

While c. above would be undeniably the best choice, allowing both giver and receiver to feel good, a. happens far more frequently.

When I was in a wheelchair, people cut in front of me 90% or more of the time. About 5% of the time people slowed to allow me to pass, and 5% of the time they actually helped. This is by no means empirical, but I have talked to others wheelchair bound and they report similar experiences.

Did those embracing assistance waste much time helping? NO. Did they feel good about what they had done when I smiled and thanked them? YES. Why is it we instead briskly forgo helping? Is our time so valuable that donating a few precious seconds to someone else now hurts us?

Did those who scooted ahead save much time? NOPE. Did they feel good because they beat me. HARDLY. Were they ignorant, bone-headed, likely to date a slug, idiots? There goes that brain surgery again. Well . . . not ALWAYS. They were merely absorbed in what they thought was important instead of doing what was.

Manners take little time, cost nothing and create benefit beyond the deed. We feel better when we treat others better. When we stop to look beyond ourselves, amazing things happen. Staying self-involved causes us to miss the couple in their nineties, holding hands, gazing lovingly into each other's eyes, the mother and teenage son, talking and sharing time together, the cute dog being walked by the proud owner. Self absorption and self pity create tunnel vision preventing us from seeing much of what is good in life.

Smile and wave at strangers. If they don't smile back, they will at least wonder what you've been up to.

CHAPTER SEVEN – Achieve and Be Happy

Attitude, Achievement, Legacy and Satisfaction

Achievement, climbing the mountain peak, legacy, how people will see us when we are gone, and satisfaction with the manner in which we lived life, make us happy and are worthy goals.

Attitude

A positive attitude can change desolate sand to lush green gardens. The first step is the belief that bringing water to the desert will make things grows.

The tree house was going to be tough. Anna's Dad had agreed to construct the playhouse when she was only four. He had been far less busy back then. Now that she was a big girl of eight, she was hopeful that Dad would fulfill his promise.

She had asked him just last weekend if they might work on it together. He had sighed, smiled, and, remembering his promise, agreed to start the following weekend.

Tomorrow was Saturday. Dad had worked the previous three Saturdays. There were fewer employees now and Dad had to work more hours just to keep up. Would Dad keep his promise?

Bright and early the next morning, when Anna looked out her bedroom window, there stood Dad with wood, tools and a great attitude. He was ready. Anna threw on her clothes and ran out toward the big tree hovering over the backyard fence.

They agreed that the tree house would be relatively low on the trunk of the tree, just high enough that Anna could see over the top of the fence, but low enough that her dolls would not be afraid to enter. Dad was thinking that even at eight, she was still his little girl. Lower was better.

Anna helped for the first two hours, but, as happens with children, she grew tired of the tedious business of making sure it would not fall. Dad continued working till dark. After Anna went to bed, Dad brought out lights so he could finish the job.

The next morning, Anna again looked out her window. There in the tree, about five feet above ground, was a beautifully constructed tree house. A rope ladder, obviously the entry, hung from its bottom. A rope, with a bucket attached to its end, hung from a window. The bucket was on the ground, ready to be an elevator for dolls and other important stuff. Dad stood next to the tree admiring his work.

Anna ran out the back door, hugged her dad's leg. When he bent down to hug her back, she kissed him on the cheek. She was very happy and so was he.

"It's beautiful, inside and out," said Anna.

"But you haven't seen the inside yet. How do you know it's pretty inside too?" he asked.

"I know it's beautiful," Anna said. "You built it and it's full of love."

Anytime you wake up and see the ceiling, it is going to be a good day. A positive attitude allows us to tolerate things that would otherwise be intolerable. A good attitude allows us to recover from life threatening surgery, even when everyone tells us it is impossible.

I should not have recovered as quickly or as well as I have. But, I didn't know any better. One hundred percent recovery is the goal, even when everyone warned me that the chances of such success were very small.

Good attitude wins races, overcomes adversity, and gives us an edge in anything we try. Like I continue to remind you, our brains are stupid. They believe what we tell them. If you think you can win, you have a better chance of winning.

When medical possibilities have been exhausted and the only thing left is positive thinking, even cancer has been conquered. That is not to say that it happens all the time, but even if it happens occasionally, why not give it a try. In fact, why not try positive thinking and a positive attitude all the time? What have we got to lose?

Achievement

Achievement is praiseworthy only when effort is required. The swift can occasionally win without help, but they can only beat the best through training and repetition. When something is too easy, we can't feel good about succeeding. Without challenge there can be no pride or sense of accomplishment.

Dumbing down, allowing those refusing effort or lacking ability to achieve, demeans accomplishment. Some claim that allowing lesser achievement aids self-worth.

Who are we kidding? We all know when someone else is letting us win. The compassion and heart of those allowing us to win are in the right place, but we should never feel good about forfeit victories.

The good news is that achievement means different things to different people. All but the seriously infirm won't feel good about waking up in the morning. It is a good thing, but for most of us requires no effort.

On the other hand, if I could shoot a 90 on any standard length eighteen hole golf course I would feel really good. That would require a lot of effort on my part, learning the game of golf, and probably a lot of luck. Heck, if I could score a 90 on a mini-golf course I'd feel good, but a professional golfer wouldn't feel the same way.

In order to achieve, we must have something worthy of achievement. We will discuss priorities in a later chapter. There are some exercises in to help you define for yourself worthy goals. You will need goals if you hope to be happy.

No Excuses

When we bump into things that slow our progress, there are two ways to handle it. We can jump over the hurdle or we can make excuses about how high it is or how tough it is or how scary it is. I have a comment for that. NO EXCUSES.

We all have the skill necessary to accomplish what we set out to do, otherwise we wouldn't consider doing them. I'd like to fly, but I'm pretty sure if I jumped off my roof and flapped my arms as hard as I could, I would still break my ankles. I'm not about to try that.

On the other hand, I'm pretty sure that I could learn how to fly a small aircraft. If I stand around making excuses for why I cannot fly instead of hiring a flight instructor, then I don't really want to fly all that badly. Then, it is a sure thing I will not fly.

Legacy

Some would like a statue erected in their honor in the city of their choice, but statues are chunks of rock or metal on which pigeons do their business. They are not always the best legacy.

What is Legacy? It is actually pretty simple, even when we try to complicate it.

Legacy is doing or creating something that lives beyond our lives.

Inventors build legacy by creating something we need. Chemists concoct legacy by discovering medicines to cure human ills or potions to make life easier. Politicians leave legacy through leadership by example. Teachers, coaches and writers imbue legacy by providing knowledge and guidance that will last lifetimes. Artists and athletes create legacy when leaving behind something inspirational. Philanthropists grant legacy by donating to worthy causes.

How about the rest of us? What about us common, ordinary, meager to moderate income, with moderately or poorly bestowed talents? What can we leave that will be our legacy?

We must first dispel the notion that legacy involves thousands of people. That would be nice, but affecting even one life is legacy. Every life matters, every human being is a person worthy of attention.

If we raise our children in the best manner we can afford, if we volunteer and do a good job of coaching, teaching, ministering, treating, or simply spending time with others, we are leaving a legacy. Think for a moment about one nice thing someone did for you. If you can think of even just one, like the lady at the Portland airport, they left a legacy.

The smallest kindness that someone else will remember, is a legacy. Doing nice things constantly, a Mother Teresa, will be remembered and revered by society, but doing tiny, almost imperceptible deeds for those who need it is the legacy of champions, and we should be as proud as winning the World Cup.

There are positive legacies that we can achieve which transcend the purely sympathetic. These are goals we set for ourselves that leave behind something more, something that requires work, sacrifice and time. We each have different talents and most legacies are created within our scope of natural or learned talents.

What are you good at doing? What do you like to do? How could you use this talent to leave a legacy? We are generally happiest when doing things for which we have a talent. We are generally talented in the things we like. Yes, we can all learn to do a bit better, but not always at a level satisfactory to us.

But, even when we cannot do, we can teach. The best coaches are often not the best performers. Gifted athletes, authors and artists can rely on their God-granted abilities. The rest of us have to work at achieving some level of competency. Who is likely to be the better instructor? The natural who never thought about being good, or the student turned teacher who had to learn how to be better?

Unfortunately, legacy has two sides. We can also choose to leave behind a negative legacy. We can harm or take advantage of others. We can allow greed to overcome virtue. We can permit anger to overcome compromise and contentment. We can use work, alcohol or drugs to hide from the world, hurting or ignoring the ones we love and everyone who loves us. We can hold or create grudges lasting decades.

Beware Shakespeare's quote "The evil that men do lives after them; the good is oft interred with their bones."

We must do far more good than evil if we hope to be remembered well. It takes little effort indeed to be remembered badly.

How will you be remembered? What will be your legacy? How many legacies can you leave behind? The possibilities are endless.

Satisfaction

I can't get no satisfaction
I can't get no satisfaction
'Cause I try and I try and I try and I try
I can't get no, I can't get no

When I'm drivin' in my car
And that man comes on the radio
He's tellin' me more and more
About some useless information
Supposed to fire my imagination
I can't get no, oh no no no
Hey hey hey, that's what I say

Rolling Stones, Satisfaction

Satisfaction and contentment, for the purposes of this section, are synonymous. Satisfaction is derived from the knowledge that we are, we have or we accomplished something that is worthy. Satisfaction is personal. Satisfaction is individual. Satisfaction can be assisted, but cannot be guaranteed by anyone else.

There are many who subscribe the theory that everyone should set goals beyond their means as a way of stretching. Setting lofty goals may overcome limits we mentally set for ourselves, and that is good. There is also wisdom in setting goals we can achieve. If we reach for the stars we must be satisfied if we get the moon, otherwise frustration intervenes.

I would love to run a 100 yard dash in less than 8 seconds. That would make me quite famous. The chances of that happening without mechanical contrivance, is zero. If that is my goal, and I know it to be impossible, how serious will I be about achieving it? Stretch, but don't break.

We need to be satisfied with good, even if we don't or can't achieve great. We should be content if we put forth the effort but don't bring home the trophy. We cannot control circumstance, divine guidance, the order of the universe, luck or ability. We can only achieve what is within our timing and ability to achieve. If we give it our best effort, we should be satisfied starting the ball rolling, whether or not we are around to see if it knocks over all the pins.

However, there is a fine line between accepting what we have and striving for something better. Appreciate where you are, even when your destination is down the road. Take each measured step happy in the knowledge that your present circumstance isn't as bad as the circumstance for many.

Chances are pretty good that if you are reading this book you are not living in a mud hut in a third world country, hoping that your family will have enough food and clean water to survive the day.

We are better off than we think, even when that isn't very well off at all. Where you are is much better than where you could be, even if it is not as good as it will be when you get there. Enjoy the journey, and journey on.

A Norman Rockwell Day at the Beach – Kat Sanders

CHAPTER EIGHT – Is it Love?

Love, subservience, sacrifice and spirituality

Love is not what we believed it to be in high school. It is deeper, longer lasting and more satisfying when we recognize and embrace true love rather than succumbing to heartthrob.

Subservience does not mean servitude. There are times when being subservient is honorable, practical and necessary.

Life without sacrifice is like a cookie without sugar. You can get through it, but it isn't very good. Sacrifice helps us remember what is good and what is important about humanity.

Spirituality is necessary even if one believes in nothing. The pursuit of logical can only make sense when faith explains the unexplainable. Even those who believe in chaos and coincidence subscribe to spirituality by virtue of their belief in nothing. The belief in nothing is also based on faith, since the Godless claim there is no physical proof either way.

For me, it is comforting to believe in a Supreme Being, a father-like figure who loves me and takes care of me. I am so imperfect and my life is so fragile that there must be something more permanent and perfect than I. My near-death experience makes that faith even stronger. The odds were not in my favor, and yet I survived.

There must be a reason for my second chance. I wonder what that might be. I am determined to find out and enjoy the journey through discovery. I hope I live to be a hundred, but however long I'm given, I'm going to make the best of it.

Love

There are sappy romance novels proclaiming love to be that feeling in the pit of your stomach, or aching in your heart. Or it is described as an overwhelming wooziness every time that special someone is, alternately, around or absent. That is the love of teenagers. Have a glass of milk, eat a pickle and get over it.

Sex may be part of it or not, but true love is found in the satisfaction that you are with someone who will love, respect, take care of you. Someone who will allow you to take care of them. Someone who will be with you for a very long time, perhaps for a lifetime, maybe even for eternity.

Contrary to popular belief, love is also spiritual, sibling, parental, or friendly. It is not a feeling that arrives quickly. It must be earned and received, graciously and respectfully. The office attraction or greener grass elsewhere is seldom as good as the satisfaction gleaned from a successful, fulfilling relationship.

When I came out of the hospital, Steve had to dress me, feed, me, bathe me and watch over me. He had to manage our company, take care of our home, pay the bills, maintain contact with our many friends and family all by himself.

I don't even remember what happened in the hospital or the week or so after I came home, but I know Steve loves me.

My affliction caused our bankruptcy, resulted in the loss of our home and everything we worked together to acquire over twenty years of marriage, and he doesn't care. To be fair, he loved our home and did care that his Koi would have no place to live, but he values my life more than any of our possessions. He would rather see me healthy and 100% than win the lottery. He is satisfied with me, no matter what that looks like. That is love, and I love him so much the more for that.

Love allows us to disagree and still care. Love prevents us from harming each other, even when we want to smack them upside the head. Did I say that out loud? I didn't mean it . . . really.

Love is comfortable, warm, respectful and full of forgiveness, even when you want to smack them . . . oops, there I go again. Love **IS** having to say you're sorry, over and over. Love is enjoying your beloved even when they brush their teeth loudly or hang the toilet paper the wrong way (at least he sometimes remembers to replace the roll). Love is learning when to say "Yes, Dear," even when we don't mean it.

You know it is love when you'd rather be together for the rest of your life rather than with anyone else. Love isn't getting past the first year, making it through two years, passing the three year dulls or sprinting around the seven year itch. Love is more laughter, friendship and sharing than sex.

Love is living the truth, infatuation is often living a lie. I'm not implying that sex is not important, but it is the sprinkles on top of the icing on top of the cake. A nice addition, but without the cake, would be far less satisfying.

If you want to be happy you have to love and be truthful, whether it is your God, your family, your friends, or your significant other. You cannot love inanimate objects or work. They will never love you back and love must be mutual.

You CAN love a pet. Many people prefer their dog or cat to their partner. If you find that to be the case, get a better partner. Wait till you cool down, though.

Love/hate decisions made in haste don't tend to be lasting. If love, effort and attitude fail to produce the level of commitment desired, step back and evaluate both where you are and where the relationship is.

Through my malady, we discovered that love is sacrifice in addition to that warm and fuzzyheaded feeling. If you aren't willing to help putting on underwear or help them into a bath, if you can't picture yourself kissing them, even when they aren't at their most attractive, you have something less than lasting love.

Steve promised God that he would take care of me, however I came out, **"just please let her live."** That was quite a commitment at the time. My prognosis was not good. My chances of living through the surgery were iffy. Even after I survived surgery, they weren't sure if I would breathe on my own, be able to talk or walk or even feed myself. They said I could be a vegetable, a cripple, blind, deaf and/or dumb.

They didn't know how the brain trauma might affect me. The fact that Steve was willing to take me "however I turned out" is true love. I'm so glad I turned out so much better than expected, because it enables me to be a better wife to him, and do more to show him that the love is mutual.

Subservience

Hopefully, no one reading this is involuntarily indentured, but if you are, RUN. Sorry. Had to do that.

Subservience and slavery are two very different things. A subservient manager knows how to make employees feel wanted by serving coffee themselves or by cleaning up after a meeting. A subservient employee gets coffee when asked. All of us should be more willing to be subservient, as long as it is not abused. Subservience is beneficial when voluntary, but becomes a bitter pill if expected or demanded.

Servant leadership is the type most admired, but not the most feared. Theory X management, "Do it because I say so," rules through fear and power, not by example. Servant leadership requires leaders to lead by example, generally embracing consensus.

If we have religion at all, then we believe there is power greater than ourselves and must submit. Unless, of course, you are the Supreme Being. If that is the case, I'm sorry for interrupting and please don't strike me with a bolt of lightening. I don't like thunder or lightening.

Subservience is knowing what we know, but also admitting what we do not know or control. This was hammered home when I fell to the floor with my bleeding brain.

Sometimes we are better off when being subservient and admitting we do not have control, even if a control freak like myself. There is nothing more frustrating than worrying about or trying to control something over which we have no control. The lottery numbers are going to come up, whether or not they are yours. You cannot control it so why worry about it?

Worry, within bounds, is normal. Whether expressed or not, good parents always worry about their children, even if they are thirty-five, healthy, wealthy and wise. However, allowing worry to take over will not lead to happiness or fulfillment.

Submit. Release. Let go. Have a cookie and a glass of milk. Get on with the rest of your life.

However, subservience does not mean living under someone's heel. Occasionally we must submit even when we don't think it is a good idea. A requirement that we always submit, except from our Supreme Being, is wrongfully imposed by the dominator.

America is supposed to be a classless society. No, I don't mean that America has no class, but I do mean that we are all born with equal opportunity. There are those in America who have put themselves above the law or bought people who can protect them from the law, but that does not make them better than the rest of us.

There is no one destined by birth to be better than anyone else. All citizens in America have the opportunity to become the person of their dreams, to rise above the ashes from whence they came. Subservience must be voluntary, not involuntary servitude, to be effective. Good leadership earns the right to lead, bad leadership forces others to serve.

Sacrifice

I'm not talking about burning virgins at the stake here, I'm talking about real sacrifice.

"Take one for the team." "Be the sacrificial lamb." "Be my wingman."

There are dozens more expressions representing the concept of sacrifice and it generally falls into two categories. Sacrifice one thing in our lives for something of equal or better value. Sacrificing something we cherish for the benefit of someone else.

Do you sacrifice your own time when running Jenny to softball practice or Jacob to piano lessons? Have you forgone a vacation because Alicia needs braces or grandma wants to see Disneyland before she dies? Have you given up a career you cherished because your spouse was transferred to another state? Have you taken time away from your personal pursuits, volunteering instead to serve breakfast for a non-profit fundraiser or ringing a bell to collect donations? Have you sacrificed by volunteering at the church, synagogue or temple? Have you served on a non-profit board or given money to a worthy cause?

Sacrifice, like forgiveness, is difficult. Giving what you can easily afford is not sacrifice. Giving up something dear, pennies when you only have a dollar, time when you have none, is sacrifice.

Like other good deeds in life, we are never quite sure, at least immediately, that the sacrifice was worth it. We may have to wait hours, days, months or years before thanks, acknowledgement or fulfillment result. The thanks may never come. It is not the ultimate reward or thanks that is important, it is the act of atonement, the giving of the gift, the sacrifice, for its own merit, that is worthy of praise and contentment.

Those willing to give for the greater good have their heart in the right place. Those always looking out for "ME" have much to learn about happiness and satisfaction. Giving of ourselves results in happiness.

Spirituality

I can just picture Yoda saying, "Transcend the physical world, we must."

In Star Wars films to the date of this book, Yoda has not said this, but he could. Mr. Lucas, feel free to steal this quote should you so desire. I give it freely as I mean it freely.

The esteemed Mayo Clinic espouses positive thinking as a way to heal more quickly and maintain life balance. The Mayo suggests that positive thinking and positive self-talk will result in:

■Increased life span

■Lower rates of depression

■Lower levels of distress

■Greater resistance to the common cold

■Better psychological and physical well-being

■Reduced risk of death from cardiovascular disease

■Better coping skills during hardships and times of stress

There are numerous medical studies supporting this claim, so there is something, even if we don't know what to call it, beyond the physical. It has power. Use it.

If we do not make time, probably every day, for individual private introspection, we are risking our health and well-being. Call it what you like; prayer, meditation, reflection, private down time. This time away from the physical world is necessary for centering, coming up with solutions to life's problems, asking for guidance from powers beyond ourselves. It is the time we need, away from menial distraction, to ponder the most important decisions facing us.

The form, methodology or ritual matters little as long as such pursuits are meaningful to you. Sure, I would rather have you subscribe to the same beliefs and rituals that I do, because I believe them and have seen them proven. However, the number of people in the world that have beliefs different from mine far outnumber those who share the same ideologies and I'm okay with that. Belief and faith work differently for each of us. They are as individual as we are and cannot be coerced.

You have probably already defined your own spiritual path and if it works for you . . .good. If you have no path, or you do not take time to pursue the spiritual, it may not kill you, but it is not helping either.

Terrorists, insanely believe that their own salvation can be derived from the pain of others. That is probably not a good spiritual determination. Praying to anyone or anything to justify what we want is not the same as listening to the response.

Common sense, morality, and the conscience possess small, but persistent voices. If you have to talk yourself into something by removing internal moral restraints, it is a good sign that what you are trying to justify is probably not a good idea.

Giving yourself time to focus on something other than immediate physical or mental need brings greater peace. We all need something outside our physical selves and should spend time searching or exploring.

Those who have no direction should spend time finding one. Those who do should spend time learning, studying or reflecting on what they believe to be true. Acts of mental celibacy for short durations can provide contentment, even if for only those few moments.

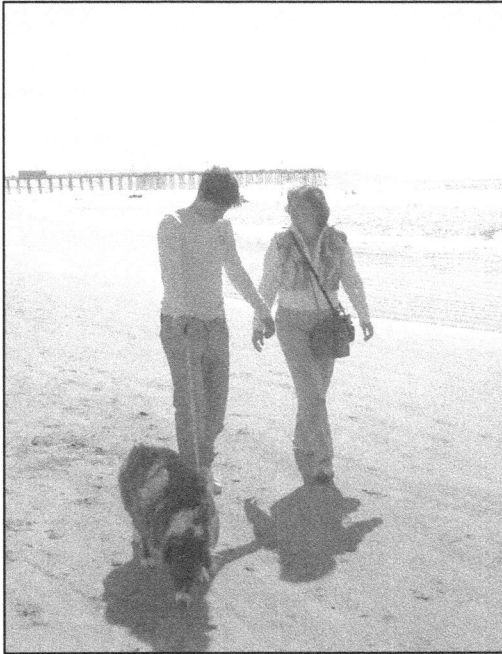

Kat, Son Matt and Brandy in Pismo Beach

CHAPTER NINE – What Do You Know?

Learning and knowledge

Knowledge, even for knowledge sake, can be good. Despite the dire predictions of science fiction literature, in which man is always concocting his own demise, the search for knowledge has provided mankind most of its greatest breakthroughs.

Imagine how Edison felt when the light bulb finally burned. Think about Graham Bell and what he must have been thinking when Watson said "Hello" for the first time.

Researchers like Newton, Galileo, Da Vinci, Pasteur, where doing research to overcome a problem or societal convention or scientific anomaly. Their research for knowledge sake seldom had dollar signs attached. Though, one should not be quick to discount the power of the pecuniary. Modern research is often well funded, with huge financial upsides, and provides as much public benefit as bang for the buck.

Regardless of the reason, Knowledge is Power. If you know more about your business, it gives confidence that you can ply your craft with the best of them. That builds confidence, which leads to greater success, which leads to more business.

Learning a musical instrument, once required of every high school graduate, can give hours of pleasure when correctly plied. Of course, hours of pain often result for the unintended family audience while the instrument is being learned.

Learning to write . . . God knows I need help with that one (but I mean well). . . results in books, long heartfelt letters or blogs that benefit writer and reader alike.

Hobbies of any kind, that require skill and knowledge, become more worthwhile the more we know. We need to devote the time necessary to hone the skills that sooth the soul, but not at the expense of living. We cannot spend the family fortune on fishing trips if we need the money to survive. But fishing can be done at little cost in the nearby lake or stream. Find a way to do your hobbies without sacrificing the comfort of others or damaging your relationship.

I'm not yet sure about bungee-jumping, skydiving or parachuting. Rather, I am sure that you'll never get me to do it, even if you tell me it is fun. Jumping from or out of something, without flames nipping at my heels, seems silly and frankly scares the heck out of me. But, if that is what works for you, more power to you.

Don't knock it till you've tried it? I've heard that before and am sympathetic to the sentiment. We should not preclude possibilities that will help us grow or make our life more fulfilled. But this is one of those cases where we all have to choose what is right for us without enduring the pain of error. I'm pretty sure I wouldn't like driving my car into a brick wall so I think I'll avoid trying it.

Four warning caveats about knowledge:

1. Not everyone wants to hear what you know, even when you just have to tell them.

Most of us have a passion about something that we like to talk about, and that is good. Controlling or taking over a conversation or training is bad. When you see eyes glaze over, or you've been talking for ten straight minutes without taking a breath, or you've run out of things to say about your fervent topic, you've probably gone too far.

Though I have not had occasion to feel this way often, many women are afraid to look "too smart". Steve is extremely smart and isn't afraid that I will somehow demean his position in life or marriage, just because I too have a brain. Though after my brain surgery it is true I have less of a brain than I did before. The ice cream scoop took some of it away.

There are husbands, bosses and friends that would rather we be cute and dumb. To heck with that. You're going to have to accept me for who I am, and I choose to be smart. I intend to use all of the brain I have left.

2.   Know-it-alls don't want to hear it at all and some are afraid that you might look better than them.

Unless you like arguing, there are some people better left ignorant. If they think they already know it, and you tell them they don't, the only possible outcome is conflict. Correcting a know-it-all is like setting fire to a gas can. You can do it if you choose, but the outcome could be a loud bang.

There are others who are afraid that your knowledge will show them up, that you will look better or smarter than them. Yes, they should grow up and appreciate you for the knowledge you possess, but that happens less often than you might think.

3.   If what you know is harmful or dangerous to someone else, take a while to think about how you will deal with the consequences of disclosing such knowledge.

When you find out your friend's husband is cheating on her, if you find out your boss has a secret offshore account in the Caymans, to whom do you go, where can you run, what should you do?

This is the purview of conscience and doing the right thing. If the knowledge you have must see the light of day, then it must, even at the sacrifice of immediate happiness. Happiness will only come in time with the knowledge that you did the right thing. But, if the truth is unnecessary or will be discovered in short order through the natural course of things, or will likely do more harm than good, think twice.

Honesty for honesty's sake is not always good. If your best friend asks you how a dress looks on her, and she is truly looking for advice (like in the dressing room) give the advice gently and thoughtfully. That is place for input, not after the dress has already been purchased and worn. Often, such answers must be measured carefully, regardless of 'Truth.'

The excuse "But it's true," doesn't resonate well if the tone or truth is unnecessary, hurtful or angry.

There are times when withholding honest comment would be the preferable course of action. Exceptions should be few and far between. Honesty may not always be the best policy, but it is generally a good idea. If withholding truth is not harmful to the whole, not harmful to you, your friends or family, then it may, I repeat, MAY, be acceptable. Will the truth or knowledge do greater harm than good if known?

However, when withholding truth or telling lies is beneficial to no one but you, step back and evaluate the benefit thereof. If someone did find you out, what might be the outcome? If you don't tell and are caught lying or avoiding the truth (same thing) what might happen? How will you feel about yourself if you don't fess up?

It is a surety, in this imperfect world, that truth will often be punished and that reward will go to those willing to lie and cheat. That is the way of the world and nothing will change that. I am certainly not saying that is how I prefer it to be, I am simply acknowledging that is the way it is. Since I've apparently lost some of the filtering ability I once had, I now sometimes speak before I think. I'm more inclined to say it like it is. Not always a bad thing, but I do prefer thinking it through – when I remember to do so.

Whether Yin and Yang, good and evil, God and Devil, Id and Ego, there are sides to each moral dilemma and you are free to choose which side you are on, just as you are free to tell whomever you want whatever you want. But you have to live with the consequences of those decisions.

4.   People often shoot the messenger.

In ancient Rome, generals sent messengers to the enemy, requesting parlay, asking for mercy or to deliver a message. Often the response was execution of the messenger. Not much has changed. If you are the harbinger of bad news, you will be punished. The best way to avoid being metaphorically killed is to have private conversations, one-on-one if possible, explaining the situation, seeking quiet and agreeable resolution.

Let's move onto what choices are actually yours to make and how to make them.

I'm All Ears –Kat Sanders

God gave us two ears and one mouth, so we could listen twice as much as we speak.

CHAPTER TEN – What Are my Choices?

How to decide what is right in my life

While it is true that goals change as life changes, many of our core desires remain for a lifetime. Let's discuss what types of goals may be best for us. We'll call them Life Goals. Achievements of Life Goals make us happy and content with our lives. Failures to achieve Life Goals make us sad, or disgruntled or wistful.

What Life Goals are NOT

Though power itself is probably not a Life Goal, ascension to becoming President of the United States might be, depending on the motivation for wanting to be President.

Many mistakenly believe that power will bring happiness. Power over others is the antithesis of feeling good about ourselves. Forcing others to do what we want results in anger, rebellion, hurt feelings and all the other negative emotions contained in the human arsenal.

Manipulation falls into the same category. In our heart we would always know that a coerced choice was not a choice at all. How could anyone feel good about that? How could that be a Life Goal? Power for power's sake cannot be good. Allowing others to make their own decisions, educating them so they can make informed judgments then enjoying their good choices, creates happiness.

Money is crinkly, dirty paper containing the germs of strangers. Money, for its own sake, is not generally a goal, it is the means to an end. It allows us the freedom to do what we want. What happens if what we want to achieve doesn't require money. How important would money be?

Though numismatics (collectors) value money for its collectability or scarcity, most of us want money for what it can buy or do. Given the opportunity, we would all like to be rolling in dough, surrounded by our mansion and eight cars, but money itself is not a Life Goal.

Material possessions are the quicksand of life. They cause us pleasure when we first achieve them, but generally cause pain later. As newness wears off or the possession is broken we feel badly. When we can no longer afford the payment, and collectors make their inevitable calls, we certainly don't feel good. Fear of losing the possession causes . . . well . . . FEAR, and fear is not good. When someone takes our possession from us, we don't generally rejoice.

Though a possession can be a Life Goal, like a house or a classic car, we must always be vigilant. If the possession possesses us or causes strife, we must decide whether or not the possession is worth the hassle. If you are blessed to have a life partner, talk about your goals and see if you can agree on some of the major ones. It's much better to share a goal and work together to achieve it, then to achieve your secret goal only to find that it causes your partner pain or disappointment.

Even knowledge can be a questionable commodity. Are those with a PHD any happier than those with a high school diploma. Is a literary agent in New York happier than an illiterate farmer in Ecuador? Education and knowledge cannot cause happiness, though knowledge may be necessary to achieve a Life Goal. Besides, knowledge for its own sake can be fun, like learning to play the piano or bridge.

Steve is a font of useless knowledge that he has gleaned over many years. You would want him on your Trivial Pursuit team. Too bad, so sad, I always get first dibs for him to be on my team,. I stink at Trivial Pursuit, so I need him. He has a nearly photographic memory and remembers much of what he reads. He used to read school textbooks the night before the exam and still aced the tests. Not fair, I know. Nevertheless, he's always fun to talk to at a party, spouting his poems, stories and wisdom of the interesting but not-very-important facts in life.

Knowledge can be important. Most of us would prefer that their surgeon had studied at least one medical book or more, but knowledge, by itself cannot guarantee happiness. Just ask Adam and Eve.

Time Matters

President Abraham Lincoln, at Gettysburg on November 19, 1863 said, "The world will little note nor long remember what we say here but it can never forget what they did here."

Here is a life truth, whether or not we choose to listen. We are not what we say, we are not what we promise to do, we are whatever we spend our time doing. Our time on earth is limited, for some of us more limited than we imagine, spend it wisely.

If you spend most of your time in bars or beneath a bottle, you are an alcoholic. If you cannot find time for your family or loved ones because work calls, you are a workaholic. If you spend four hours a day playing video games, you are a gameaholic (I made that up too). You get the point. Don't say one thing, then do something else. Don't waste time on the trivial if you haven't gotten where you need to go.

I get it, I really do. Right after brain surgery all I wanted to do was sit around. I had no desire to do much of anything but sleep. Steve got me up and around for a few minutes each day and day by day I stayed up longer, did more and felt better, but had it been left to me, I'd still be sitting on the couch drinking my Ensure (vitamin supplement) with a bendy straw and hugging my cat.

It is far easier to drug ourselves with TV, the internet, games, or actual drugs or booze, than face the world. Eventually you will have to get it going. Why not spend some down time thinking about or working toward that end goal instead. If you are spending more time lying around than accomplishing your bucket list, what are you. Right, a lay-around-at-home-ic (another made up word-don't you just love it?).

Unless you spend time doing what you say you want to do, it is obviously not yet a high enough priority for you. Before my surgery I was a workaholic. Post surgery you can bet your tush that I am spending my time more wisely.

For example, Steve and I went to one of my favorite parks near the beach. We sat at a picnic table, each with a pad and latte, and talked about upcoming trainings, goals and what we intend to do with our spare time. We could have been in the office, but why? Why not be where we want, regardless of what we are discussing.

In fact, much of this book was written at a park, or in our backyard watching the sunset, or at least in our family room, sharing time together. My little Bengal kitten curls up on my lap as I type. That's living.

Insignificant choices made everyday affect our quality of life. Why not make them with a focus on better spending the precious time we have left on earth?

I was complaining about the cell phone being a bothersome leash when our friend, Jason, overheard and told us his story. He was lunching with his wife at a nice Newport Beach restaurant, when the cell phone rang. Much to his wife's chagrin, he answered the call he had been waiting for all morning.

She good naturedly teased him about being a workaholic, to which he responded, "This was a very important phone call I had to take. I could have waited for the call in the office, or I could take you to lunch at a nice restaurant at the beach and take the call when it came in. Of course, I'd rather be here with you than at the office." Then she felt a little silly for teasing him.

This is a demonstration of the power of choice. If you have a choice of taking the call while dining with your spouse, don't wait at the office. I am getting much better at that. However, if attempting romance, let it ring, or turn it off for a while for Pete's sake.

My 10 Best Days

We have all had days that stand out, days that we remember regardless of what we are doing or where we are today. Seldom, unless you have won the lottery, is it about money. What was it about those days that stood out? What made them memorable?

Determining what is memorable about them allows the good experiences to be repeated. Also, how much time did it take? Was it all day or just a few hours? How much time or planning would it take to repeat?

Steve and I have two favorite days that cost less than $10.

Day 1

We were taking a trip up the California coast and went through the 17 mile drive in Monterey. Steve packed a picnic basket with an inexpensive bottle of wine (probably around $4.00 in 1990), a couple of sandwiches, some fruit and, this is the most important ingredient, a box of Bugles. Bugles are kind of like a corn chip shaped like a little funnel. They have a taste similar to, but not exactly the same, as a Frito.

We spread the checkered tablecloth on top of some big boulders overlooking the ocean. We unpacked the rest of the food including the Bugles, and ate while we enjoyed the view. I knocked over the box of Bugles and some tumbled to the rocks below. We only lost a few, no big deal.

We were pointing to objects on the horizon, trying to discern the type of boat, fish, swimmer or buoy with bare eyes, when I felt a

tap on my leg. I looked down to discover a very fat squirrel looking at me with the same begging eyes my cat gives me at breakfast. I jumped, scaring both the squirrel and myself. I have never before had a wild animal walk up and touch me.

The scary, woman-eating squirrel was on one side of me, and a thirty-foot drop to the ocean below on the other. Okay, it was a cute, harmless fat squirrel, but it took a few seconds for me to weigh my options.

Steve saw me jump, but didn't know why. As I was explaining, he burst into laughter and began pointing at something behind me. Sitting just out of reach was the fat squirrel, standing on his hind legs. I threw a Bugle in his direction. Almost as quickly as it hit the rock on which he stood, he grabbed and ate it.

In a few seconds he was back. As I started to throw yet another Bugle, a second little squirrel head popped up from behind another rock. Then a third and fourth squirrel appeared. By the time we finished lunch and the Bugle box emptied, we had at least ten squirrels enjoying Bugles. Some of them were even bold enough to take the food out of our hands.

As we finished our wine, watching the sunset, the satiated squirrels made their way back to homes in the rocks. The fullest of them would have trouble squeezing back into their narrow confines, but all were happy. It was a simple, wonderful experience, but it would be right up there in the top ten of my best days on earth.

Day 2

For a few months we lived on the Central Coast of California. A beautiful and relaxing place to live. We were within 30 minutes of Hearst Castle and decided to make a day trip and take one of the tours.

For those unfamiliar with Hearst Castle it is in San Simeon, California, on a bluff overlooking the ocean. It has some of the most inspiring gardens and landscape in the state. The artwork and furnishings inside the facility are truly magnificent. It is one of the must see places in California if not the U.S.

The facility is managed by the California State Parks Department. A limited number of visitors are allowed each day. Steve, my son and I were there one weekend and the maximum had already been reached, so we could not take the tour. Disappointed, but not disheartened, since we could visit nearly anytime we wanted, we took a drive up the coast.

We were about seven miles north of San Simeon when Steve pulled the car off the highway into one of the many view turnouts dotting the road. As we pulled in, an attendant wearing a blue coat stepped up to our window and asked, "Are you here to see the elephant seals?"

Steve turned to me and we looked at each other quizzically. Elephant seals . . . what is an elephant seal, we wondered?

He turned back to the docent and hesitantly said, "Yes . . . yes we are looking for the elephant seals."

She directed us to a cove turnout about a half mile down the road, an area called Piedras Blancas. There were probably fifty or more cars parked there. We got out of our car, cameras in tow, not knowing what to expect.

An elephant seal is a large ocean mammal of the genus Mirounga. An adult male can be 16 ft in length, weighing over 5,000 pounds. The female is much smaller and can be 10 to 12 feet in length, weighing in as large as a ton (2,000 pounds). Approximately 75 pounds at birth, pups grow to 250-350 pounds in less than a month. The normal nursing period is 25-28 days. Though relatively passive if left alone, bulls become dangerously aggressive when their territory is encroached. They are pretty funny looking and have snouts like an elephant.

I have never been formally trained with a camera, but Steve, who has, says I have a good eye. If he says so (and he would never lie to me). Actually, it must be somewhat true as I am constantly asked if the photos at home and in our office are professional reprints. I just love to capture life and sometimes the beauty comes through.

When we arrived at the boardwalk, overlooking the beach approximately 10 feet below, we could see hundreds of elephant seals in the rookery, for that is what it was. Every year, these elephant seals come back to the same place to bear and rear their young.

Though once endangered, protected from hunters by the state, they have multiplied and thrive off the Central Coast. Though difficult to know how many actually visit Piedras Blancas, since they are not all there at the same time, it is estimated that as many as 8,000 elephant seals use this location.

Mother elephant seals nursed and prodded their young as male adult seals looked on. It was the photo op of a lifetime. The beach was perhaps three quarters of a mile in length and every foot had a seal on or somewhere near it. If you like animals, it is a must see. Did I mention how funny looking these tons of fun are?

I took several memorable photos. We traveled back to Pismo Beach, had an early hamburger dinner and drove home. It too was a great day, where we laughed and shared the unplanned and unexpected experience as a family.

I chose these two best days just to demonstrate that memorable days aren't necessarily important days. Our first date was incredibly romantic, and we celebrated our wedding day with one hundred of our closest friends and family. We were married at sea on a pirate ship. When the ceremony was complete, they fired cannons. These were both great days, but took planning and resources. The example days I used were pure accident

We should learn to make and take good days whenever they happen and acknowledge that they can be a complete accident rather than the result of extensive planning.

Buccaneer Queen – Kat and Steve's Wedding Ship

CHAPTER ELEVEN - Fun, Passion, and Talents

Having Fun

Doing what we can to have fun makes our lives happier. When you are out with friends or playing catch with your child or you've just smacked a 300 yard drive (like that could happen to me), that's fun. Sitting on the boat, the wind in your hair, or driving the coast with the top down (hopefully in a convertible), that's fun too. There are things that cost very little that are joyful and we don't take advantage of them because we believe they will always be there. I have proof that is not the case.

TAKE the time to do fun things. MAKE the time to do fun things. Don't put them off till it is too late. Children grow, pets get old, stamina diminishes. Do whatever you can to do it NOW.

Most of us will agree that the fun things in life are . . . FUN. But what about everything else? What about the chores, responsibilities and work. Those comprise the bulk of our day. What can we do about all that time spent on activities that are not fun?

MAKE THEM FUN!

Steve worked at Disneyland when he was in college (just a couple of years ago). He tells a story about an employee of Disney that found a way to make his job fun. Ride operators put people into the Matterhorn, Pirates of the Caribbean and all the other attractions at Disneyland. They remind you to "stay seated and leave your arms and hands inside the car at all times." The job is repetitive, rife with crowd control conflict and can be boring.

There was a ride operator working the Matterhorn, while doing his job effectively, who learned to do the "Robot" dance while delivering required instructions. Guests found it amusing and actually paid attention. The ride operator got pretty good at mimicking a robot and worked at getting better each day. He had a good time and so did everyone around him.

The original Jungle Cruise script at Disneyland was entertaining, but pretty tame. It wasn't till ride operators got hold of it and, in an effort to make their job more fun, that it became VERY entertaining.

Later, Jungle Cruise ride operators entered a contest sponsored by management, to see who could come up with the most entertaining script. Some of the off-color scripts were not Disney approved, but many of the best submissions were incorporated into a new script.

Drudgery or Challenge

In everyday life, there are things we all must do that we don't necessarily like. We have a choice of making them horrible experiences or changing them around to be more fun.

Basic household chores are not the highlight of my day. Scrubbing toilets is not something I look forward to or dream about. But, if I turn on some upbeat music, dance and sing my way through the chores, I forget about the drudgery because I'm focusing on the fun. My neighbors probably think I'm trying out for Idol because I sing really loud.

I can do leg and toe lifts while cleaning the sink. I can bend over and touch the floor with my palms (Yeah right, let's just do fingertips) as I 'm picking up things on the floor. I can aerobicize my way through the day and combine exercise with work. That is much more fun and makes me THINK I'm doing something good for me whether or not that is true.

When I have a lot of paperwork to do, maybe paying bills, organizing files or reviewing contracts, I try to do it where I can enjoy myself. One of the benefits to having a completely electronic office is freedom to make that choice.

My office is wherever my laptop happens to be. I find a pretty park or beach, plug in my aircard (or tether my computer to my phone) and spend a few hours in a beautiful place. I bring a stale loaf of bread to share with the squirrels and birds who stop by.

A word of caution here. Don't feed seagulls, doves, black birds, pigeons or crows. If you feed one you will soon have a flock, and they are messy. They don't care where or on whom they let go. Squirrels and small birds are much less hassle and you don't need a hat.

Children can alternately be rewarding and frustrating. A show of hands please . . . all of you who enjoy changing dirty diapers, please raise your hand. Anyone . . . anyone?

This is a chore that nobody likes, but could you distract yourself by imagining this messy child graduating from college or completing his or her first brain surgery, taking their first step or hitting that first home run? Teach them a song while you wipe their bottom. It might be entertaining for both of you.

Again, I remind you. Your brain is stupid. It will believe anything you tell it, even if imaginary. Cook up the best stories you can think of about your kids before they get old enough to stick their tongues and interrupt your fantasy.

Another word of caution here. The minute children turn thirteen, parents become extremely stupid. Whatever it is you thought you knew, they know you don't. Steve and I have a theory. The minute they become teenagers, their glands swell, blocking all blood flow to the brain. They are unable to think again and can only accomplish what their hormones will allow till they turn twenty-two or more.

Girls mature more quickly than boys, and some men never grow up. Just look at my husband, Steve. Decide for yourself.

Keeping the right attitude will help you have a happier life. Don't focus on the yucky tasks. Reward yourself constantly – then you can look forward to the reward. How about a nice glass of wine and a bubble bath? Or ice cream. Did I mention I like ice cream? It is the perfect food. Find a way to make the necessary evils in life more fun.

Passion

Though sex can be included in this discussion, passion is more than a roll in the hay. Passion dictates the direction we lean, whether we choose that path or not. Please don't confuse passion and talent, they can be quite different. We discuss Talent later in the book.

Passion is internal, free from the encumbrances of rationality or ability. They are the things we do when no one else is watching. They are the activities we desire that no one else is required to approve or rate. We do them because they make us happy.

I have a passion for the arts, pretty much all of them; performing arts, dance, visual art, music . . . I was fifteen when my first song was published. I even got a check . . . not a very big one, but HEY! I can even carry a tune respectfully. It is an obvious intersection of passion and talent.

However, as I may have said before, I cannot draw. I'm really good with layout and page arranging, but if I painted a dog you would think it was a cat, or worse. I did find that I had a pretty good eye with a camera, so I do my art through a lens. A few of my pics are in this book, so not too bad.

My point here is find a way to do what you love. If you do, you will be successful and happy. If you don't, you will be unhappy about it later.

This does not mean quit your day job. While I was a television producer I volunteered to help with the local civic opera. I was also president of the board of a women's shelter. You can always find a way to help in the areas of your passion, even if you don't have the talent to do it yourself.

Is there something related to the talent that you could do? Steve was a talented baseball player. I've never seen anyone, professionals included, make the plays he used to make. A bum knee kept him from going pro.

Now that he is older than dirt (did I say that out loud?) his dream of playing in the big leagues is irretrievably lost. But, he can, and sometimes still does, coach. He may still get into a slow pitch game now and again, against my sound advice, but his playing days are largely over. We go to a professional game at least a few times a year and he enjoys watching the young bucks butt heads while we drink beer and eat hot dogs. He still enjoys the game but is realistic about his abilities and is happier because of it.

That reminds me, passions can change. Steve used to play ball four to five days a week and played tennis too. Today that would probably kill him, and if not would certainly maim him beyond the ability to carry on. As we age, as other talents and interests grow, our passions may also change. Continue to reassess what is important, at least yearly, perhaps more often. Make sure the road is mapped before heading down it.

What can you do that satisfies YOUR passion that is both realistic and possible? If reaching the pinnacle is your measure of success, disappointment is likely. I'm telling you to give up. Be realistic and happier with the level you are capable of achieving. Luck and opportunity often have more to do with reaching the top than ability, but you can still achieve happiness below the summit.

Talent

Steve once coached a Little League player who had very little athletic ability, but loved the game of baseball. He knew every player on every team. He memorized all the stats. He could describe the best batting and pitching stances even if he couldn't do them himself.

As a player he was destined to ride the pine (a sports term that means he would be sitting on the bench instead of playing). Even at the Little League level he would be one of the players to be named later. But, as a father and baseball coach, he would later excel.

If you have talent, find a way to use it. If you have passion, but no talent, find a way to get involved with the passion.

How do you know if you have talent? Most of us know what we can do well and what we cannot. However, most of us tend to downgrade talents we have, either as an attempt at modesty or because we truly don't see it. If you have doubts, but want to know, ask someone who is an expert.

Ask a music or art teacher, or writing instructor. Ask a coach. Be prepared for the response and know where it is coming from. Experts on *American Idol* go beyond honest, their frankness closer to mean, because there is entertainment value in "Telling it like it is."

Don't ask someone with little patience or concern, but do ask someone who will be straightforward. Your friends may not give you the answers you need. They may be a poor judge of your talent or may be afraid of hurting your feelings. Ditto your parents.

Parents are seldom going to tell their progeny that they are terrible, but they may say things like, "That was pretty good. Have you thought about water polo?" or "Honey, with a few years of lessons you could play Carnegie Hall."

Enter a contest or two and see how you do. Again, be prepared. Just because one set of judges doesn't like your work, others may.

Stephen King, a voracious professional writer of many years, had a tough time making a living as a writer. After many years of writing with little monetary success, he wrote a short story entitled Carietta White. After a few short pages, frustration overcame passion and into the trash it went.

Fortunately for all of us, his wife Tabitha, retrieved the discarded manuscript and convinced King to complete it. The book, Carrie later sold for $400,000 and King received half. It was also made into a successful movie. He quit his day job as a teacher and the rest, as they say, is history.

Even when others doubt you, if you have a passion, follow it through. Find the time to pursue the dream. Balance the dream against the need to survive and do what it takes to learn and thrive.

However, don't sacrifice all of the good in life, including family and friends, to reach a goal. Stepping over others, just to get there, will not be good for you in the long run. The top can be a lonely place when everything and everyone else is buried at the bottom. Getting there, and still having a life, will bring you a mountain of happiness.

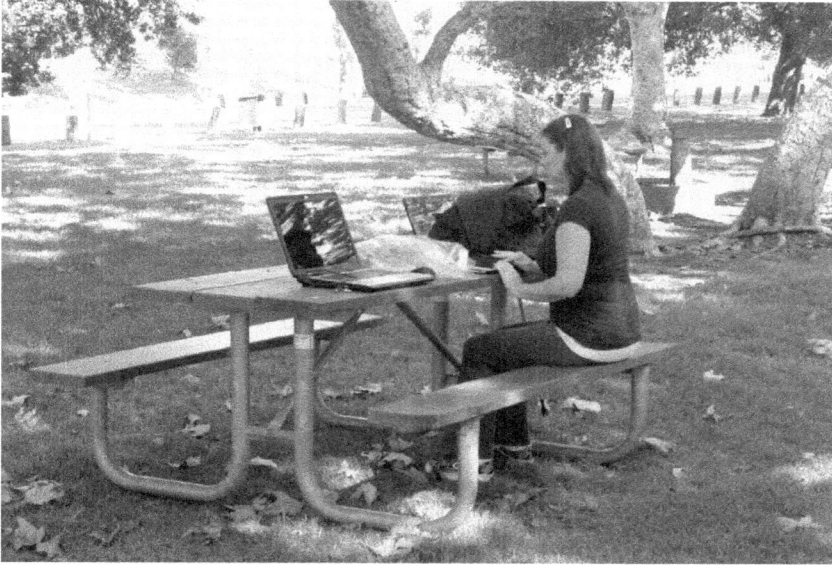

Kat Working in the Park

CHAPTER TWELVE - Exercises

The below exercises are designed to draw out hidden desires, goals, aspirations and talents. Knowing all of that is key to learning what in life is important to you.

If I Won the Lottery

What would I do?

For the next few minutes, sit down and write the 10 things you would do if you won the lottery. In addition to the things you would buy, what would you DO with your life? Teacher, researcher, explorer, leader, traveler, writer, painter?

1. _____
2. _____
3. _____
4. _____
5. _____
6. _____
7. _____
8. _____
9. _____
10. _____

What we would do, outside the world of economic constraint, is always a good indicator of what is important to us. The responses to this exercise should point you in a direction that is important to you in the long haul.

Bucket List

The ten things I want to do before I kick the bucket.

1. _____
2. _____
3. _____
4. _____
5. _____
6. _____
7. _____
8. _____
9. _____
10. _____

What on this list are you working toward? What has the highest priority? When do you plan to be there? If these things are truly important, will you schedule the time and resources to do them? If not, they are wishes, not goals. On my list is taking my grandchild to Disneyland. I don't have a grandchild yet, and am not necessarily in a hurry to become "grandma," but I know I would love to someday have the opportunity.

Million Buck Give Away

If I had a million dollars to donate, name 5 people or organizations and how much each would get.

1. _____ $ _____

2. _____ $ _____

3. _____ $ _____

4. _____ $ _____

5. _____ $ _____

This indicates who or what organizations are most important in your life. Are you volunteering or spending time with them now? If not, why not? What is stopping you?

What is my Legacy?

How Do I want to be Remembered?

Imagine you are writing your own epitaph. What would you want it to say? Name five things you want people to say about you when you are gone.

1. _____

2. _____

3. _____

4. _____

5. _____

Ten Best Days Exercise

Now make a list of your **Ten Best Days**. Unless you are younger than 10, If you can't think of 10 days, or after writing the list you see four or five lame days, there is something out of balance in your life that seriously needs change.

1. _____
2. _____
3. _____
4. _____
5. _____
6. _____
7. _____
8. _____
9. _____
10. _____

What Am I Passionate About

Make a list of the things you absolutely love to do. Don't let time or money limit your choices. Starting at the bottom, compare each on the list with the activity above it. Decide which of the two you would rather do, then move that one up the list. Repeat the procedure till you have your entire list prioritized. Then write down the top five. Those are your passions.

1. _____
2. _____
3. _____
4. _____
5. _____

What Are My Talents?

Though we all want to think we are capable of doing anything, and frankly that is a good attitude, there are many things that will require extensive training to achieve a level of competency. We need to know the difference.

Learning to better do what we already can is going to take less time than learning to do something well that we presently have no talent for doing. It is not a matter of will or knowledge. It is a matter of time.

There is also the remote possibility that one may not have what it takes. If I want to be a singer, but am tone deaf, that is going to be a challenge indeed and may not happen. If I draw pretty well, but cannot figure draw, that is trainable over time.

Talents I think I have	Talents that Others Have Identified
1. _____	1. _____
2. _____	2. _____
3. _____	3. _____
4. _____	4. _____
5. _____	5. _____

Now that you are all done doing your personal assessment of what is important, let's take a moment to reflect. Look at what you would do if you won the lottery. Look at the list of people or organizations to whom you would give money. Scan the bucket list. Glance at your ten best days. Are there commonalities, things that appear or are related to things on one of the other lists?

Your Comfort Zone, Goals and Legacy

Pastor Rick Warren, author of the best selling book *Purpose Driven Life*, says "If you're alive, there is a purpose for your life."

All of us are meant to accomplish something, whether big or small. Until that is found and accomplished, we will intuitively feel that something is missing in our lives. You now should have a pretty good idea of what that might be. Now all you have to do is decide where to go with it and how to get there? Keeping in mind that there might be something in store for us that is off our radar screen, the following chapters will help organize and direct priorities we already know about.

Things I need to Say

Pretend today was your last day on earth. Make a list of the things you need to say and the people to whom you need to say it.

What I need to say?   Who needs to hear it?

1. _____   1. _____
2. _____   2. _____
3. _____   3. _____
4. _____   4. _____
5. _____   5. _____

Don't leave important words unsaid. Tell them you love them. Tell them what you hope for them. Tell them you forgive them. There are thousands of parting words, and most have significant meaning. Don't wait till it's too late.

Sunset in BC

– Kat Sanders

CHAPTER THIRTEEN – Priorities

Let's Get Going

If you completed the exercises in the previous chapter, you probably have a pretty good idea about what is important. It is a truism is that if you fail to plan you plan to fail. Just knowing where we want to go doesn't help if there is no roadmap. After doing the exercises ourselves, more things changed. Steve and I both love animals, and wildlife. So spending more time feeding the ducks and squirrels at the park and getting out in nature will create more opportunities for great experiences. So you will likely find us at a local park working instead of sitting in the office. Technology is great and has helped us "live" better.

As I said before, I have been, admittedly, a workaholic. The one thing Steve and I did right, before I went on the forced workaholic detox program, was Date Night. Friday night was Date Night and nothing was allowed to interfere, even if all we did was watch movies on the TV at home.

We discovered that even being nice to each other and spending quality time together had to be scheduled or it didn't happen. If we allowed it to, and I did, work could absorb every precious moment available.

Even when we know what is important, how do we determine what is first and what is last in order of priority? How can we organize so we miss nothing? That reminds me of a story.

Big Rocks

A professor was trying to teach his geology class about mountains and how they came to be. He explained that they must be built on a solid foundation, else they would wither away to molehills. He explained that there was a priority to the compiled foundation and that only the proper order of organization would result in longevity.

Chapter 13 - Priorities

He had in front of him a large empty container and three smaller containers. One of the smaller containers had several big rocks, another had pebbles and the third had sand.

"The goal," he said, "Is to get all the contents of the smaller containers into the big container, and, like many natural phenomena, I have to get the lid back on, constraining the elements. Failure to do so will result in an unstable mix."

"Which element should I put in first?" he asked the class.

There were several shouts from the attendees, finally the instructor said, "Raise your hand if you think the smallest particles, sand, should go in first."

Sixty percent raised their hand. It made logical sense. Put the smallest in first so it left more room for everything else.

So he poured the sand into the large empty container, and asked, "Since you started with the smallest first, how many of you now think the pebbles should go in next?"

Emboldened by their instructor's apparent acceptance of direction, even students who were initially fearful, raised hands high over their heads. Eighty percent believed they were headed down the right path, selecting pebbles next.

In went the pebbles. Last, then, were the big rocks. They would not fit. Not only could he not get them in, but the lid would most certainly not close.

Disheartened students let out a sigh of resignation. There must be a lesson here somewhere.

"Let's try that again," said the instructor, separating the three elements back into their original containers. "Let's start with the big rocks."

The big rocks easily fit into the empty container. The pebbles, poured in next, worked their way around and under the big rocks, also easily fitting into the container. The sand, placed in the container last, sifted between the pebbles and big rocks, filling in all available space. The instructor then took a glass of water and poured it over the top before easily closing the lid.

"Not only did we fit all of our elements into the container, but we also managed to add some water. This is the foundation for lasting geological structure," professed the professor.

Lest you mistakenly believe that I made this concept up, I must confess that it is stolen. Big rocks, and the realities they represent, are an ancient Zen teaching. In a Japanese garden, big rocks represent life's immovable mountains. It is unusual to find more than one large stone in a Japanese garden as more than one would be a complication. You probably have more than one big rock in your life, but that stands to reason. Our lives are complicated.

There is wisdom beyond geology here. If we start with the big rocks in our lives first, everything else can be fitted to them. What are your big rocks?

Big rocks are the things we discussed in the previous chapter. They are the events, people, things to do, that make life worthwhile. They are the choices, without which, life cannot be fulfilling.

For those with 8 to 5 jobs, mark out 8 to 5 every day. Before adding overtime, decide if the bucks are worth the cost of missing birthdays, recitals, Little League games or soccer matches. Will you have more gain by attending the school play or making a few extra dollars?

Now go back and decide which days you can afford to take off and MARK THEM DOWN. If you fail to schedule it will not happen. You will forget to ask for or take the time off. You will fail to find someone to cover for you. You may even forget the event or outing all together. If it is in black and white, it will remind you.

If you have the ability to schedule your work time or are self-employed. Mark down the important stuff first. You cannot affect the time or place of a football playoff, but, much of the time, you can schedule your work around it.

Name five big rocks in your life

1. _____

2. _____

3. _____

4. _____

5. _____

Now arrange them, most important first, then schedule them. Put them on the calendar. Do this at the beginning of each month. Add to the list as something comes up.

If you are married or have a significant other and romance is not on your list, you are in big trouble, Bubba. Romance requires forethought and planning.

If you hope to keep your partner happy, you'd better put in some time, and appreciate your partner when they make an effort. As we discussed before, you are what you do, not what you say. Saying I love you a hundred times is not as effective as planning one special date.

It doesn't matter whether you are male or female, the responsibility for romantic planning is the same. Don't complain about lack of love if you don't make the effort. If they don't make you feel like a million bucks, what have you done to make them feel important. The door swings both ways.

The Bucket List

Things to do Before I Kick the Bucket

Remember the bucket list. Create a long term plan for achieving those goals. Write them down. Hang them on the wall, frame them. Put them on your to do list, where you can see them everyday.

Remember, our minds are stupid. They believe what we repeatedly tell them.

When we spend time planning a special trip or event, or imagine ourselves in the home of our dreams, our mind thinks it is real. When the brain thinks something good is going on, it produces serotonin, dopamine, acetylcholine, phenylethylamine, or oxytocin, natural brain drugs that make us feel better and stronger.

Thinking good is good. Spend time planning for realization of the bucket list.

Look up cruises and imagine going on them. Research your favorite city, putting yourself there mentally. Pretend you are lying on the beach, enjoying your pina colada, soaking up the sun. Whatever is on your bucket list, look it up, think about it, read about it. The more you do, the more likely it is to happen and the better you will feel even if it doesn't happen as soon as you would like.

The anticipation of reaching a goal also helps us to stretch and admire how far we have come. Striving for something important makes us feel important.

When the prize is finally within reach, grab it, don't blink. Trust me; there may not be a tomorrow.

Now Do Something!

By now you should know what you want and what is important. But, all the planning in the world means nothing, if you do nothing about it. Plans without action are like wheels with no traction. You will spin in place and go nowhere. Besides, as we discussed above, getting there is half the fun, so get on the road.

Take little steps. If money is the stopping point, start with a jar of coins. Put that in a special bank account. Instead of buying an expensive sandwich or cup of coffee, take your lunch or coffee with you one day a week and put the money you saved into your special account. You will be surprised how quickly it mounts up, if you don't steal from it.

If time away from the job is required, how many days do you need and how do you accumulate the time? Do you have to change or accumulate vacation or job swap? Do you need to train someone to temporarily take over while you are gone? Can you set yourself up to do what you need to do while still on the road?

Whatever you need to do before doing what you want, can be started now.

Balboa Sweet Success – Kat Sanders

Action Items

List 10 Action Items you can start today that will lead to accomplishment of at least some of your goals.

1. _____
2. _____
3. _____
4. _____
5. _____
6. _____
7. _____
8. _____
9. _____
10. _____

If there are more things you could do, schedule them, but be careful. If you have more Action Items than you can readily accomplish, you will get frustrated and frustration seldom leads to happiness. Take small steps.

What else do we need to be successful on our new ride? The following chapter will bring it all together and provide a way to make it happen.

CHAPTER FOURTEEN – I've Got the Idea. Now What?

First let's set some ground rules for ourselves.

Patience

If it doesn't happen exactly as scheduled, relax. Reschedule for a different day. It is there to remind you, not nag you. Whether you accomplish your personal task on Wednesday or Friday doesn't matter nearly as much as accomplishing it, period.

I am an impatient person by nature. Those who know me will tell you, "No Duh!"

But I have had to learn patience through my second chance. There were times when I cried because I wasn't as sharp or quick as I used to be. Everyone who knew about brain trauma, Steve included, told me to be patient. I still fought.

Fighting, to a point, is good. The will to get better will help you get better. But, fighting to the point of frustration slows you down and makes you crankier. Not a pretty sight.

My doctor told me I shouldn't drive for a while because my depth perception was off. I decided I could drive (remember I have no patience), so I tried it out in a parking lot. I ran over a curb. Doc was right. I couldn't drive. So instead I'll enjoy having a chauffeur for awhile. If only Steve would wear one of those cute chauffeur hats, it would be even better.

Rehabilitation, whether life or injury, is a process. It takes strength, the ability to bear pain, work, but mostly patience. We cannot overcome extreme change, injury or surgery overnight.

Steve had two hip replacement surgeries. The first was difficult. He wasn't sure how quickly he would heal, he didn't know what to expect and he was extremely impatient.

He wanted to do all the things he could do before, and more, and he wanted it NOW. He couldn't sleep normally for about a week, he couldn't sleep on his side for about three weeks, till the stitches came out, and he couldn't walk or stand normally for about six weeks. Full recovery took about six months.

After the second surgery he was far more patient. He knew what the timeframes would be, knew what he could and could not do. He was still impatient, but not nearly as bad as the first time.

There is a reason Alcoholics Anonymous has a twelve STEP program. Healing of any kind happens over time and in measured steps.

AA's 12 steps.

1. *We admitted we were powerless over alcohol—that our lives had become unmanageable.*
2. *Came to believe that a Power greater than ourselves could restore us to sanity.*
3. *Made a decision to turn our will and our lives over to the care of God as we understood Him.*
4. *Made a searching and fearless moral inventory of ourselves.*
5. *Admitted to God, to ourselves, and to another human being the exact nature of our wrongs.*
6. *Were entirely ready to have God remove all these defects of character.*
7. *Humbly asked Him to remove our shortcomings.*
8. *Made a list of all persons we had harmed, and became willing to make amends to them all.*
9. *Made direct amends to such people wherever possible, except when to do so would injure them or others.*
10. *Continued to take personal inventory and when we were wrong promptly admitted it.*
11. *Sought through prayer and meditation to improve our conscious contact with God as we understood Him, praying only for knowledge of His will for us and the power to carry that out.*
12. *Having had a spiritual awakening as the result of these steps, we tried to carry this message to alcoholics, and to practice these principles in all our affairs.*

Much of the above can be applied to recovery from any physical or mental injury. It is also a good way to heal misdirected life.

Recognition of an issue or injury must come first, then a request for help, then the slow healing process. Many people trivialize the malfunction, failing the first test of recognition. Others expect that injuries caused by years of neglect can be fixed in a day. It is a process, a journey, enjoy it.

Steve constantly reminded me that the brain heals slower than a hip. I never asked him to jump hurdles or run the mile while he was recovering from hip replacement surgery, why did I expect my healing process would be quicker? Patience . . . patience! I'm working on it.

Partnering

None of us is very good at being our own boss. Few of us would fire ourselves, but that, or a swift kick in the behind, is often what we need. Partners provide a good method for congealing our chosen direction.

Partnering is exactly that, holding each other accountable for meeting or following chosen directions. A partner is not someone hired to tell you what to do. A partner is someone you trust who has chosen a tide similar to yours, needs help riding their wave and is willing to help you get the most out of yours. They are also there to pick you up dry you off and help you get the sand out of your wetsuit when you wipe out.

A partner doesn't have to be a spouse or significant other, though it could be. It could also be a friend or family member. But, if your significant other is trying to make the same changes you are considering, it would be better partnering up and gently reminding each other about the direction of your wave. Not because a significant other is better or worse than any other partner, but because successful experience as a couple creates life bonds that will bring you closer together.

Have them work on the same exercises and buy a book (please have them buy another book, I beg of you). You need to be on the same page (so to speak).

Rules for Partnering

Rules . . . we don't need no stinkin' rules. Au contraire. Without rules in advance, partnering can become a battleground instead of a field of play.

Call a Time Out

There are times when ego or anger gets the better of us. We need to put ourselves, and our partner, in a timeout till that passes. Have an expression or word that calls for a break. Take a predetermined time out, an hour or more, to cool down before resuming the discussion.

Misunderstanding

Communication is tough enough without trying to guess what the other person means. Our assumptions about what was said or meant, are wrong far more often than we want to believe. If they say something that hurts, ask them what they mean before assuming that you know. We are our own worst enemy and often take what others say or do in the worst possible light. Clarify rather than guessing.

Right Words, Wrong Words

Words like Always, Never, Hate, especially if linked with the word YOU, are to be avoided. In fact, the word YOU often implies knowledge or experience that may or may not be accurate, since using that word often implies that we know what the other person is thinking. Sadly, clairvoyance is not yet perfect. The ability to read others thoughts, and perfectly understand what they mean, remains illusive. Avoid "YOU" as much as possible. Stick to "I" which you know much more about.

Be a Coach, not a Mentor

Passing on business knowledge and teaching students are appropriate venues for mentoring. Personal relationships and partnering are not. Mentorship implies subservience or inequality of knowledge. Partnering does not. Partnering is more like coaching. Good coaches don't dictate; they convince and encourage. The best coaches are the ones who not only know what is wrong, but can help fix whatever that is in an encouraging manner.

You must be willing to let your weaknesses show. You can't fix the problem until you identify it. In my case, my tendency to worry was making life less happy. Admitting that to Steve and asking him to help me worry less was difficult to do. Of course, he was already aware of this minor issue. He has known for more than 20 years. But, he was gentle about admitting that knowledge and was wonderfully supportive in offering to help me overcome the problem.

I do worry less now. Of course, when you're no longer worried about death and the afterlife, it becomes much easier to worry less. But don't tell Steve that – I want him to think he helped cure me from worry.

Handle Conversations with Love

Criticism is criticism, no matter how well intended. Suggest, kid, and assist, but do not cajole, criticize or demand. Treat your partner as though you are a teacher talking to a kindergartener. We may be mentally above that level, but emotionally we are all still schoolchildren. And everything is more palatable when offered with a smile, a hug and/or a kiss. Chocolate works too.

Scheduling

I know this is where I'm going to lose some of you. Few of us like to impose restrictions on ourselves and scheduling our lives feels like a restriction. WRONG.

Scheduling is also creating freedom. In addition to scheduling what we have to do we also get to schedule what we want to do. Scheduling reminds us that we missed or might forget something. Scheduling allows us to plan for down time, free time or play time.

Scheduling reduces duplication. Which is more embarrassing, writing down your activity for Saturday night, so you remember, or double booking?

Scheduling, good. Forgetting, bad.

Where Do I Start?

Whether using a scheduling program, Outlook, or a hand-written calendar/task list, schedule the action items. If it isn't scheduled, the chances are pretty good that it won't happen. It's human nature.

I am a founding member of Procrastinators International (I hope there isn't a group with that name already). If it can be put off, I'll find a way. Many of you are also members, even if you don't know it, or don't want to admit it.

How Far in Advance do I Plan?

Though many of our Big Rocks are likely to be somewhat futuristic, and may be years away, they are already on our mental list. It is best to plan for a year in Quarterly increments, but no longer than that. Write down your annual Big Rocks, then break them into achievable Quarterly accomplishments.

There is a school of thought that setting reachable goals diminishes our abilities because we are no longer stretching, reaching for the stars. Unachievable goals create frustration. Stretch, but do not break. Reach further than you might otherwise, but understand the difference between Hope and Dreams.

After you've written down the quarterly goals, break them down into weekly goals.

Plan to set aside time to plan!

Big Rocks First

Get the Big Rocks and priority actions done early in the day. Otherwise procrastinators like you will get away, since they also wait till later in the day. Forcing yourself to act as quickly as possible (without being rude-don't call before 9:00 AM) will resolve procrastination. Working early will result in a more effective day. After all, the early bird gets the worm. Yuck! Well, maybe it's a gummy worm for us humans.

Fill in with Pebbles and Sand

With the Big Rocks already scheduled, it is easier to fill in the rest of our week with superfluous, but otherwise necessary stuff. When putting in the sand and pebbles, schedule the "have to's" first and the "want to's" last.

Make yourself a promise to achieve as best you can, but don't beat yourself up if you don't. Achieving 100% of anything is not possible all of the time.

Schedule at least an hour a day for nothing. This allows you to have down time, move things around, or seize opportunity. Opportunity seldom happens on schedule. We need the time to take it and run. Plan that open time in advance.

Be Prepared to Make Changes

Nothing ever goes as planned.

Steve and I were heavily involved with drama. We were playing an aging husband and wife (further from the truth back then). The lead actor uncharacteristically missed his cue and remained off stage. We were making small talk on stage for the benefit of the audience, trying to cover up his delayed entry.

Suddenly he appeared on stage with a panic-stricken look on his face. He looked down at his lapel mike, which was tangled in the gauze around both hands. In a previous scene his character had burned his hands rescuing someone from a barn fire. We saw his predicament.

Instead of waiting for him to come to us, which is how the scene was written, we made our way to him on stage. I was playing his mother, so I hugged him and stayed close enough that my lapel microphone could pick up his voice. His speech was loud and clear to the audience. When he finished his soliloquy, we made our way off stage, as written, where the stage crew could fix the problem.

We taught our drama students that the occasional onstage gaff is never an if, it is a when. We need to be prepared for it. We are not judged by the error. We are judged by how we respond. Be prepared and adapt.

Hammer or Tool

Goals, and the schedules we create to achieve them should never be used by ourselves or our partner to hammer us. They are a tool for guiding how we want to live and should be used as such.

I'm a workaholic with no concept of time. My partner, Steve and I have agreed that no business will be done after 6:00 P.M. Occasionally, things will come up that require bending the rule, but not as often as before. When 6:00 P.M. rolls around and I'm still on my computer, Steve will turn to me and ask, "You're not working are you?"

I always reply, "Noooo . . . no, I'm not working." And either quickly close the lid to my computer or seek out a computer game to play. Usually I go to Bejeweled. I like it and I'm pretty good at it, though I was better before surgery.

When Steve forgets the 6 PM rule, I like to tease him by saying "you do know what time it is, don't you?!?" He is more honest about admitting his forgetfulness, but he likes to beg for a reprieve sometimes. We barter over the cost of the reprieve, and I usually score pretty big, getting extra kisses and extra household chores done. It works and it reinforces the importance of family over work.

If partnering, gently remind your partner about the rules you both agreed to without hitting them over the head with them. A soft touch generally results in better a better outcome. Everything is better with a smile and a kiss.

By now, you should know what you want, you have a tide chart/roadmap for getting there, and you have a partner to help you if you lose your way. From here on out it is up to you.

Checkups

Schedule (there's that word again) weekly sessions, probably no more than an hour, to go over the week with your partner. Talk about what worked, what seemed to elude you and get feedback about how happy you seemed to your partner.

If you schedule weekly meetings, save non-emergency critiques for that time. Handle crisis as it occurs, but talk about everything else at the weekly checkup. Doing so will eliminate the feeling of constant criticism that comes with significant change.

Congratulations. You are well on your way to successful living. Now just a few final thought before you catch the wave to your new life.

I'm Not Lion. Trust Me - Kat Sanders

CHAPTER FIFTEEN - Affecting, Changing & Accepting

In order to achieve happiness we must become realistic. We need to know the difference between personal preference and reality. Forcing our priorities on others would be dictatorship and not well received.

Freedom is freedom. We have to take the good with the bad. There will be people and convention we will not be able to directly change. We may affect them, by taking moral or personal stands, but we must understand that we cannot make them do what we want.

Our goals and happiness cannot rely on someone or something else becoming something different from what they already are. While we should strive to affect change, when change would be good, change often does not come in our lifetime.

Those who know me well know I love polar bears. Not because they are fluffy and cute, but because they represent how we treat our earth. I know that change in environmental attitude is necessary for our Earth to thrive. I applaud the efforts of many who have peacefully and cooperatively changed how we do business to better protect our fragile biosphere, but we have a long way to go.

My ultimate desire would be that we are doing what we can to maximize efficient use of resources. That desire cannot be a reasonable goal. I can never know what that means.

Science and what we do to the world is changing ever faster. Goals of today mean nothing given what we might know tomorrow. Because the concepts are always in flux, and largely theoretical, I will never be certain that we are doing all we can. If my happiness depends on that certainty, I will never be truly happy.

However, I can be happy if I help affect that change. I can be happy teaching others to be efficiently green, or teaching them to better treat themselves or others. I must be happy affecting change, without having to see the end result.

I have a friend whose husband doesn't treat her very well. She is and has always been in love with him, even when he cheats on her. She always says that her happiest day will be the day he discovers he cannot do without her and treats her in a way that reflects that respect and love. Right!

Children are pliable and readily changed. Their habits are in flux and can be affected by teachers, coaches, peers and parents. Adults are less flexible. Their habits are far more firm and change can only happen when they decide to change. If your happiness relies on a leopard changing its spots, your happiness may be a very long way off and may never come at all.

We must decide how to best deal with the important people in our lives without the expectation of changing them. If the relationship is so fraught with frustration that meaningful change is required, distance from the relationship may be a good solution.

Or, change expectations. If we expect less from others and accept them for who and what they are, we can be happier, but only if the way they treat us is good for us.

Inconsiderate smokers bug me. I used to smoke and gave it up as a teenager, realizing that it was a harmful, expensive habit I could not afford. Smokers who respectfully smoke away from others, outside or in their own car, have my humble appreciation. Those insisting on smoking next to me do not.

Since my lung collapsed, I have had some trouble breathing normally. Smoke, that before did not affect me, now brings on convulsive hacking. In restaurants, casinos, stadiums or other venues that allow smoking, I am in imminent danger. In the past, I often have to avoid these venues altogether.

I understand that I affect smokers' freedom by hoping they will smoke elsewhere. But they keep me from doing many of the things I want to do, just because they cannot wait to get outside to smoke.

I have two choices, I can take precautionary steps, like a mask, and do what I want, or I can avoid doing what I want to do. I have to ask myself which of those two will make me happiest and sometimes that changes. What I cannot do is wait for government to protect me by making everyone stop smoking.

Actually I've stumbled on a more elegant solution. I have a small fan that fits in my purse and I can blow the smoke back at them. Cool, huh?

Most of us do not have the legal authority to make people do what we want. Even government has trouble enforcing what is law, otherwise there would be no need for court or jail. The expectation that we can get others to do what we want can only frustrate us and make us unhappy. Acceptance of the things we cannot change and avoidance of the things we cannot stand, will lead to a more satisfying existence.

Spend more time with the people you find most consistent with your lifestyle and less with those who insist on being toxic. The nurse and parent in all of us want to make changes, even when they are unlikely. Instead, hang out with those who already make you happy, and tell them so. You cannot say I love you enough.

When I finally became cognizant, after surgery, I realized I hadn't done that. I wasted time worrying about things I could not change. Worse yet, I failed to let others know that I value them. I will tell them I love and appreciate them more often.

Daughter Kristi - Ready to Ride the Wave

I no longer hope to change people, even my family. I hope to affect them, and will attempt to do so with kindness. I am happy I now know the difference.

Banff Springs Hotel – Kat Sanders

CHAPTER SIXTEEN – Bring it on Home

AFTERTHOUGHTS

There are a few things that I either forgot or didn't fit neatly into one of the chapters, but they are worthy of mention.

Believe it or not there has been a decided beneficial side benefit in how Steve and I get along. His patience level has improved and we talk a lot more about things we need to fix.

Also, I have a new tool in my arsenal. When I've done something silly or simply want to get my way I point to my head and say "Brain Surgery." He smiles and I get my way. It is so cool. You should try it. Oh . . . I guess it won't work unless you've had brain surgery.

As a side note for those of you dealing with brain trauma, the injury can cause social side effects. After much research and discussion with many trauma victims, families and medical practitioners, they all agree that the people they knew are not the same after brain trauma or a near death experience.

Brain trauma victims might bump into walls or into people (I'm getting better and the bruises are healing), or they might not remember your name or what you said a few seconds before. Be patient with them. Maybe like me they had an ice-cream scoop take away some of their common sense.

Some have revelations that last a lifetime. Others recognize that their past is not the future they want. Like us, priorities can change for the better. But, the change isn't always good.

Victims are often more outspoken, occasionally leaning toward Tourrette's symptoms, or they can be less patient with themselves or others, or they can demonstrate severe melancholy, breaking down in tears for no apparent reason. They can pick their nose or scratch where they shouldn't in public. Modesties may disappear. Be prepared and be kind. It isn't their fault.

It Isn't Your Fault

The biggest "Ah ha" I had was that many of the things that happen to us are not within our control. Why then can't we STOP BLAMING OURSELVES?

For the longest time after my AVM trauma I blamed myself for not being a better spouse, for not helping with our business or home. I blamed myself for our bankruptcy and loss of our home. I shouldered the responsibility for my weakness and lack of balance. I kept apologizing to my husband for the horrible experience he had dealing with my brain trauma, all the sitting around at the hospital, and dealing with a less sensitive me. Steve repeatedly admonished me, reminding me that I didn't ask for a bleeding brain. But I wasn't always listening.

Please, listen to me now. **IT ISN'T YOUR FAULT**.

I guarantee you, I didn't lift my hands to the heavens and say "Please, God, strike me with a bleeding brain. I want to see what it's like."

It happened, it was painful and an experience I hope never to repeat, but it wasn't my fault.

Those of you still blaming yourself for something that happened, over which you had no control or influence, and those of you who made a mistake you now regret, place your right hand on your forehead.

HEAL, I SAY HEAL. IT'S OKAY.

There. You are cured and forgiven. You never again will blame yourself for whatever that was. Move on.

Never give up Hope

There are some who claim that the ability to reason sets mankind apart from the animals. Others argue soul, or opposing thumb, or ability to love. My cat, Nemo, has all but the thumb. He loves me. Sometimes, he can figure things out and remember better than I can. I can't prove the soul for either myself or him, that's based on faith, but Nemo has demonstrated powers normally reserved for us humans.

It is Hope that separates us from the pack. Other creatures take life as it comes, and that is good for getting on with life. But, hope allows us to look beyond the here and now. Hope allows us to imagine what could be rather than accept what is.

Hope gives us . . . well, Hope. It makes us feel better. Remember, our brains are stupid. They believe whatever we tell them. Hope tells the brain there is life beyond suffering and pain, beyond the mundane. That makes us feel physically and mentally better.

Steve and his uncle, Doug Corporon, a medical doctor, were discussing the miracles of modern medicine. Doug said, "Never give up hope. If you can live long enough, someone will find a way to fix it."

My Dad was living proof of that. He was a cat with more than nine lives. He suffered a malady that doctors said would kill him several times over his lengthy and productive life. I was about 11 years old when he was diagnosed and doctors gave him a short life expectancy. I was 40 when the leukemia finally took him from me. That was a lot of living, that others said would never happen. His hope kept him fighting for another day, and another year, and another decade. I like to think I take after him in that way.

I remember the time he and my mother were vacationing in New York and he suffered a massive heart attack. He had been a Kaiser patient for many years and instructed the cab driver to get him to the closest Kaiser. Instead they cabbie mistakenly took him to Georgetown University hospital.

Georgetown was working on an experimental heart drug. My Dad's condition was so poor, that his only hope was this experimental drug. He took it and days later walked out of the hospital. He had several episodes like this one over his lifetime, but his hope and desire to live kept him going.

Our family moved from Southern California to the Northwest to be with my Dad in his final days in 1993. The doctors gave him six months to live. Miraculous medical scientists then discovered a new wonder drug that prolonged his life for nine years. And he didn't just survive. He LIVED. He was able to go pretty much where he wanted and do what he wanted for those years.

He was and still is an inspiration to me. More importantly, his life was a message to us all. NEVER GIVE UP HOPE.

Reality Check

Okay. Now is the time to confess. You aren't really going to go through all of these steps, are you?

FINE!

Really. I mean it. Fine. These steps are here for those who need them. Some of us already know what we want, know what is important and have a pretty good plan for getting there. All that is good.

But, if you are lacking one or more of the components described in this book, you can put any one or all of them to work. What if your goals are not as clearly defined as you like? What if your goals aren't really what you believe them to be? What if they have changed or are changing?

We all do things our own way or in ways that work for us. Adapt these ideas as you see fit, but at least give each area some thought.

Practicing What We Preach

Remember, we wrote this book to remind us about what was important and how to get there. Otherwise we would forget. Like you, we too struggle with trying to make our lives more worthwhile, happier and fulfilling. We are not perfect, nor do we expect to be, but we now have a roadmap we can follow. That and our faith will get us through.

In a Nutshell

Be thankful for what you have. Don't envy those who appear to live in greener grass. They have their own set of problems, trust me. We should enjoy the ride, because that, Faith and Hope, is often all we have.

My dream for you is to live a happy, fulfilling life with no regrets, to forgive more easily, to love more, to worry less, to truly have an Unstoppable Life.

Acknowledgements and Thanks

There are so many people to thank for this book. I hope no one is missed, but I cannot make that guarantee (brain surgery might have wiped that memory out, you know.)

Doctors and Hospitals who saved my life:

Kaiser Permanente
Riverside County Regional Medical Center

- Dr. Siddiqi, Dr. Warner, Dr. Berman, Dr. Cortez, and Dr. Sweiss whose knowledge and skill allowed me to live and write this book.
- Kaiser Permanente ER staff and Dr. Wooding, who correctly diagnosed the serious problem and took immediate corrective action that saved my life.
- Riverside County Regional Medical Center nursing staff and hospital administrator who found room for me and treated me very well.

Relatives and Supporters who's actions, support or prayers made it all possible

Beth Martin
Kristi Sanders
Bob and Ter Sanders
Rebecca Newell
Laura Schaible
Bettie Boberick
TIGAR
New Heights Church
North Point Church
Living Truth Church

Cher Costa
Ken Trefts
Matt Oleson
Maureen and Mike Parniani
Janet Hawkins
Carolyn and Allen Bertholet
PSR agents and staff
Cornerstone Church
Saddleback Church

Dedicated to My Dad
Edgar Trefts

The Unstoppable Life Web Site

For those that just can't get enough, please go to

www.theunstoppablelife.com

for more information.

You can attend or schedule a seminar for your business or group. You can see which dates are still available. Or you can see when we will be at a seminar somewhere close and stop by for a visit. We'd love to meet you. We are even more entertaining in person, at least that's what we've been told.

There are also some additional exercises and tips for how to make your life happier. Check out the downloadable forms so you can do your own planning.

Email us a comment or two, tell us a story or let us know if we are on the right track. You may even become famous in our next book or seminar.

www.ingramcontent.com/pod-product-compliance
Lightning Source LLC
LaVergne TN
LVHW011243080426
835509LV00005B/610